D1095794

A HIGHLAND YEAR

Books by the same Author

IN SEARCH OF NORTHERN BIRDS

THE CHARM OF SKYE

HEBRIDEAN MEMORIES

ISLANDS OF THE WEST

DAYS WITH THE GOLDEN EAGLE

EDWARD GREY OF FALLODEN AND HIS BIRDS

WANDERINGS OF A NATURALIST

THE LAND OF THE HILLS AND THE GLENS

HIGHWAYS AND BYWAYS OF THE WESTERN HIGHLANDS

THE CAIRNGORM HILLS OF SCOTLAND

THE IMMORTAL ISLES

WILD BIRDS OF BRITAIN

AMID SNOWY WASTES

ETC. ETC.

Ancient Scots Pine standing in Glenhui, Mar Forest.
This old outpost pine is centuries old. It shows the phenomenon of spiral growth,
its wood being thickened in spirals as an additional strength against winter storms.
The hill with snow-field in the background is Ben MacDhu.

A HIGHLAND YEAR

SETON GORDON, C.B.E.

1944
EYRE & SPOTTISWOODE
LONDON

BOOK
PRODUCTION
WAR ECONOMY
STANDARD

This book is produced in complete conformity
with the authorised economy standards

Printed in Great Britain
for Eyre & Spottiswoode (Publishers), Ltd.

LIST OF ILLUSTRATIONS

PREFACE

In this book I have endeavoured to give month by month a picture of a Highland Year, its wild life and seasonal changes.

I have written of the memories of past years, of past companions, of experiences which have been unusual in a life spent in observing and recording, with a reverence and love which are necessary to see beyond the material into the spiritual heart of wild nature.

Now, more than ever, it is necessary to turn to nature for peace of mind. The glint of a lesser tern's wings above white sands, as I have just seen them, the stately flight of a solan, the Isles rising ethereal across a blue sunlit sea—these sights refresh the despondent spirits in a world weary of war and its attendant evils.

SETON GORDON

UPPER DUNTUILM
ISLE OF SKYE
May, 1944

By some of us October is seen as the crowning glory of the year. The month is perhaps viewed at its best in the central and eastern Highlands, for here aspen and rowan, birch, oak and larch flood the glens with the glory of their autumn-tinted foliage.

If we divide the Hebridean thrush from the thrush of the mainland, and even the Hebridean dipper from the mainland dipper and the Hebridean hedge accentor from the mainland hedge accentor, we ought surely to separate the weeping birch of Loch Ness, of Strathspey, of the Tummel and the Dee, from the birch of Skye and Mull, and of the western mainland. These western birches are not drooping and graceful; they are erect, sturdy and more bush-like, as they must needs be, to withstand the strong winds and tempests that so often beset them. But arboriculturists have not the same passion for subdividing trees into separate species as ornithologists have for dividing up their birds into endless subspecies, and so the weeping mainland birch and the Hebridean birch are classed together.

After a cold and backward spring the birches of the central Highlands are sometimes late in uncurling their scented leaves. Among cold springs the coldest and latest I can remember was that of 1923. I was at Aviemore on Upper Strathspey that year during the last week of May, leaving on the morning of the 29th of that month, and as the train pulled out of the station I well remember looking at the weeping birches that clothe the face of the rocky hill, Craigellachie. The whole wood was of the red-brown tint associated with February and March; there was not the faintest tinge of green to be seen that morning, when June was only three days off. Late budding gives the birch a short flowering season and it is not uncommon for the trees to be caught by an autumn frost while yet in the full vigour of their growth. Just as fields of oats in the upper straths of Dee, Don and Spey are sometimes caught and shrivelled while the ears are still green and far from ripe, so are the leaves of the birch sharply warned that their time here is short. But birch leaves are of a tougher fibre than the heads of grain, and it needs several nights of frost to turn them from green to gold. The colour of the birch in its autumn glory is seen at its best against the dark background of many pines. The entrance to the Lairig Ghru pass in Rothiemurchus Forest is one of the best places I know for seeing the birch framed by many pines. Birches are scarce here, and that is all to their advantage when their leaves turn and when a single golden birch growing beside the clear burn that flows from the high Cairngorms stands out in glory amid the dark firs, so that it may be seen at a distance of several miles.

The aspen is a later budder than the birch and is the latest tree—with the possible exception of the ash—to come into leaf in the Highlands. But the leaves of the aspen, which tremble, 'tis said, with shame because their tree supplied the wood for the cross of Christ, are more delicate than those of the birch, and although the aspen is still bare in spring when the birch is in leaf it is gaunt and leafless once more in autumn when the birch is still in the beauty of its foliage. I wonder whether it has been noticed that the aspen leaves cease to tremble in autumn, shortly before they fall?

During a sombre day in the autumn of the year 1942 I happened to be walking with a friend in Rothiemurchus Forest, and near the upper fringe of the pines, where they grew stunted and gnarled because of the fury of the hill winds, we passed a solitary aspen, large and well-formed (for it was in comparative shelter) and so bright were its golden leaves, it seemed as though a mystic fire burned within that tree, giving it an added glory.

It is for some of us at times possible to see beyond the material form of a tree into what, for want of a better word, I will term its etheric and less gross being. One birch in particular I have in mind. It is a tree perhaps fifty years old, its stem, with almost pure white bark, straight and graceful, its branches pendulous and often shaken by the wind, for it grows on a hillside without shelter. Sometimes I have looked long upon that tree and have seen it as it were dissolve in thought and assume a new and delicate beauty not of this world. Those who have seen as I have seen will understand me and what I am endeavouring to describe.

The oak is a Highland tree, but in the Scottish glens the season of growth is too short for this tree to reach the dimensions found in England. It was from the shelter of an oak on Loch Arkaig-side that Cameron of Clunes awaited his enemy, an officer of Cumberland's army, in the days that followed Culloden. But the officer received news that on a certain day an attempt would be made on his life. He knew that whoever rode his white horse that day would be the target of a concealed opponent, and accordingly he arranged for a brother officer to ride his horse. This man, who was a Highlander although of the army of occupation, was shot dead by Cameron of Clunes, who in the failing light recognised the horse but not the rider. In the Highlands the oak rarely assumes its true autumn tints: it is almost always in full growth when frost destroys the life in its green leaves, so that in time they flutter withered and shrivelled to the ground.

It is in October that the snow-beds of the high Scottish hills are at their lowest ebb. Whether, as some aver, there is perpetual snow on any Scottish hill is a question of doubt. There are two hills which I have never seen free of snow—Ben Nevis, which is the highest hill in Scotland, and Braeriach, one of the Cairngorms.

Both of these snow-fields lie beneath cliffs, where they are sheltered from the prevailing winds from the south west. In early summer these fields are of great depth, and the snow gradually melts until, at the coming of the new snow, it is as hard as ice. I have known new snow cover the old for the winter as early as mid-September but its coming is usually in the second week in October. That autumn (1942) it was later than usual, and on the 22nd of the month, when a friend and I visited the Braeriach snow-bed there was no fresh snow upon it, although I believe the snow did arrive two days later. The old snow-bed on this occasion was considerably smaller than I had ever seen it, but was in no danger of melting.

The plants which have their home near these snow-beds have a short growing period: indeed when the snow is slow in melting, or after an unusually snowy winter, they may have no growing season at all, but may be imprisoned beneath the snow throughout the year. Phanerogams—that is the higher, flowering plants—can stand one year's imprisonment, perhaps more, but Cryptogams such as lichens or mosses are able to survive a much longer period beneath the snow. At the edge of this Braeriach snow-bed are mosses which are not snow-free once in ten years, and which, even in the most favourable season, have less than a month's growth—and that in late September and October, when there is little warmth in the air at this elevation and when there is frost, sometimes severe, at night. For the first time in my experience I found that the snow, this autumn of 1942, had receded beyond the edge of all plant growth, for the stones then exposed were devoid even of lichens, and for this reason appeared unusually clean.

Nearer to the snow than it was possible for grass to exist I found small plants of *saxifraga stellaris*, the comparatively long-stemmed white-flowered saxifrage, which grows freely on damp ground in the high corries of most of the Highland hills. But in this lonely, sunless corrie of Braeriach at a height of three thousand six hundred feet above sea level there was no time for flowers to be formed on the saxifrage plants, but only the smallest of flower buds. A little farther from the snow, but still where grass could scarcely live, was a carpet of *gnaphalium supinum*; then came the grass and, still farther away from the snow, the heather. It was interesting to see that the flower heads of the grass had been killed and whitened by an early frost before they had time to become mature. Here one was sheltered from the westerly gale which rushed across the cliffs and poured the mist into the corrie in grey columns like aerial waterfalls.

9

There were ptarmigan sheltering in the corrie, and earlier in the day we had passed a number of these birds at their favourite haunt near the Pools of Dee. The wings of the ptarmigan are white, summer and winter, and during October the pure white winter dress is gradually assumed. This white plumage serves as a protection against the enemies of the ptarmigan, the eagle and the fox, but when the early winter is mild the effect is precisely the opposite, for the birds then stand out against the dark hillsides like small patches of snow. Whether by instinct or reason they know their danger and at an eagle's approach fly to snow, if a drift should be lying near, and there alight for safety.

In the Isle of Skye, and no doubt in other districts of the Highlands also, there has been a serious increase in the number of foxes since 1939. Near my home in the north of Skye the fox was almost unknown in the years previous to the war. Now it is numerous and on one township grazing alone more than forty lambs were taken during the spring of 1941, and about the same number in the spring of 1942.[1] In Skye it is (at all events at the moment, although there is pressure being put on the authorities to alter this state of affairs) illegal to bait a carcase with strychnine for a fox. My own feeling in this matter is that strychnine is a most cruel weapon, but this, it may be said, is pure sentimentalism in wartime. Even if that be so, is my reply, there is a very important practical reason why strychnine should not be used, for it is equally fatal to dogs as to foxes. A fox may carry a piece of a poisoned carcase a considerable distance, and may leave it where a dog may find and eat it, perhaps weeks afterwards, and be poisoned, to die in great agony. A better way would be to revive the ancient and honourable Highland calling of foxhunter. Farther down the west coast there is the Mid-Argyll Fox Hunting Association which (I am writing in the autumn of 1942) is prepared to give ten shillings for each fox killed in Argyll and five shillings for each cub. It seems to me that £1 would not be an excessive reward for each fox killed: the money would be well spent, and would encourage the shepherds in their trapping and shooting of this animal.

Baiting with strychnine has sometimes unexpected results, and an instance comes to my mind of strychnine set for great black backed gulls on an island. The gulls ate the poisoned carcase, died in the sea, and were washed up on the mainland shore, where a number of the local dogs ate them and were in their turn poisoned. The estate was sued by the dog owners, and had to pay £100 damages. I feel that where so

[1] At the end of April 1944, on the evening before I corrected the proofs of this page I saw a large fox on sheep ground and heard of two more in the neighbourhood.

deadly an agent is concerned it should be used only as a last resort. I know that I shall be criticised for this statement, but too many people are apt to be carried on the current of public opinion. That fearless friend of all wild creatures, W. H. Hudson, writing of a friend of his who had been criticised, made a remark which impressed me: 'Well' wrote Hudson 'I love him—a man who has had the courage to think for himself.'[1]

I was on high ground, that autumn of 1942, in the north of Skye, and Dara the collie put up a fox which made off through the peat haggs with its brush held jauntily in the air. There are no grouse on that ground, and very few hares, and at first I wondered what the fox could have been feeding upon to keep it alive, for the season of lambs was long over, but when I thought over the matter I came to the conclusion that the animal must have been living on mice. That year there was a plague of these creatures in the north of Skye, and in the early spring our crocuses and other bulbs were eaten down to the ground by them. But, more serious, they destroyed the whole of one of our corn stacks, eating all the grain in the stack before it was taken down to feed the stock. There are few owls in this district of Skye, and it might have been thought that this multitude of mice would have attracted short eared owls to nest with us, as the snowy owl in the north of Scandinavia nests, in certain districts, only in a good lemming year. I believe that we did that summer have a pair of owls nesting on the moor, but one pair of these birds would have little effect on the swarms of mice; nor do we have as many kestrels as I should have expected. A few years ago we had a very fine barn owl, which for more than one season made its home in some rocks below the house. As daylight ebbed it might have been seen hunting the grass lands for mice, and in its coloration and movements reminded me of a male hen harrier. There may have been a second bird, but the mate, if one existed, was never seen and one day my wife found the owl dead in a cranny of the rock where it roosted. Its fate was a mystery, and no barn owls have been seen in the district since.

The season of harvest in the south is a time of warm sunshine, when it is pleasant to work in the corn fields. How different is the lot of the Hebridean harvester! He must contend against cold gales and an almost daily rainfall during the season of the reaping and in-gathering of the oats. For the last three seasons this has certainly been our lot; I think

[1] In Skye I understand that the Department of Agriculture for Scotland now (1944) offers a reward of 10/6 for each fox destroyed, and in one district the members of the township offer the township shepherd an additional £1.

1942 was the worst of the three. At the end of October scarcely a stack had been made in all the north-west Highlands, and much hay was lying out in the fields. It is sometimes said that the Highland crofter is lazy and does not take full advantage of the brief spells of fair weather. There are it is true lazy crofters in the Highlands, just as there are lazy farmers in the lowlands, but I am quite sure that the difficulties and the disappointments the Highland crofter has to contend with are under-rated by those who are not familiar with his life. As an example of what weather the Highlands can produce, let me take the example of Lochmore in west Sutherland. After wet weather throughout June, July, August and September, October of 1942 gave a rainfall here of over sixteen inches. Think of sixteen inches of rain in one month—you people who live in districts in England where the total *annual* rainfall scarcely exceeds that figure. How would you like to harvest under these conditions? We in the north of Skye had only eight inches that month, yet it was one of the worst Octobers in memory.

Most of the harvest in Skye that year had been secured by the end of October. Following a fair Sunday some of the crofters began to carry their corn an hour after midnight, by the light of the moon. Even the war, and the government's fatherly advice on the matter, have failed to induce the crofters of the West Highlands to harvest on the Sabbath Day. I did hear of one farmer who defied custom and built his stacks on a Sunday. This shocked his neighbours, as the following brief conversation will show: 'I'm thinkin', Angus, that we'll no win the Waar.' 'Indeed, Donald, and why should that be?' 'Did ye no' hear, Angus, —— has bin hairvastin' on the Sawboth: that, I'm thinkin', will lose us the Waar, right enough.'

A friend has been writing to me and putting to me some interesting natural history questions. She is a keen observer of nature and it will be, I think, of interest to set down her questions and the answers she gives to them. The first question she puts is, 'Have you ever seen a heron soaring, just for fun and not because it has been annoyed or upset?' She says that on one occasion she saw this, from her front door overlooking the river. It was a beautiful sunny day, and up and up the heron soared, in great circles, until he seemed, through binoculars, to be no larger than a seagull. At last that soaring heron, a lovely sight, drifted away beyond her field of vision. I cannot recall seeing a heron soaring. He is often seen gliding earthward, but I should not rank him high as a flier. One autumn day I disturbed a heron at his fishing at low tide in a seaweed-fringed pool. The heron flew heavily a short way out to sea, then turned into the breeze and steered his aerial course parallel to the shore and about one hundred yards from it. He was flying perhaps fifty feet above the water when I noticed a gannet travelling on the same course and flying just above the surface of the sea. The gannet over-hauled and passed the heron as though that bird had been motionless in the air. Here was seen a true master of the art of flying; the long and narrow white wings, black-tipped, were moved easily, though with great power. The heron, on the other hand, was obviously finding it hard work to make even slow progress against the fresh breeze. It is interesting that in its normal flight the heron's wings are not fully ex-tended: they droop clumsily, as though their owner found them heavy and unwieldy, as perhaps he does. And yet those wings can carry him across the North Sea, from Norway to Scotland.

The second question put to me was, 'Have you ever seen a whole family of six young kingfishers and their parents asleep with their heads under their wings on a willow branch the night before they dispersed?' My correspondent says that she saw that sight once: next night there were only four youngsters at the roost. I am afraid that I am less familiar with the kingfisher than my correspondent, for it is not a common Highland bird, although it does nest on the banks of certain streams and rivers—the lower Tay for example. In winter I have seen it on the coast of the West Highlands, flying over salt water, and its brilliant plumage was very noticeable above the cold sea. I once saw a kingfisher beside the Falls of Lora in Argyll, where the sea in a sounding flood pours from the Atlantic into Loch Etive.

My correspondent's letter ends with the description of the queerest nesting site she has seen. A spotted flycatcher chose that site, which was the jaws of a mummified pike that had been taken from the river and hung on a sapling beech. Brooding between the jaws of the pike the flycatcher hatched her eggs and reared her brood, nor could she have known that in life those jaws would have speedily closed on her and her nestlings.

Unlike the pied flycatcher, the spotted flycatcher is found throughout the greater part of the Highlands although it is nowhere common. Its swift flights from some favourite perch after insects are always interesting to watch; the bird, as it must needs be, is a master of quick turns and swerves, and its prey seldom escapes. One of my most vivid boyhood memories is the nesting of a pair of spotted flycatchers in a shallow hollow (where a large branch had rotted away) of a birch tree in our garden on Deeside. Each year, late in May, I was glad to see that the flycatchers had returned safely from overseas and were faithfully using their old nesting site. But one spring my father, in order to prevent the tree from decaying further, gave orders for the hollow to be cemented up and the flycatchers then perforce went elsewhere, to my sorrow. Although I cannot equal my friend's story of a flycatcher nesting in the jaws of a mummified pike, I once as a boy found a strange combination of nests. Overlooking a clear pool of a Highland stream a water ousel had built her domed nest and reared herb rood and that same season a pair of flycatchers, much later nesters than the ousels, made their nest on the top of the dipper's.

Writing of dippers makes me remember an interesting coincidence which I recorded. I was fishing Loch Dionard, a very remote Highland loch, in October. From the high hills which rise immediately above it a waterfall drops in a long cascade, then flows in a series of falls until it has reached a point some two hundred yards from the loch, when it disappears underground and unseen enters the loch. I had last fished this loch at the end of June (and had landed a good seatrout of six pounds) and on that day saw a dipper fly up the loch and mount diagonally across the heather, taking a short cut for the falls where its nest no doubt was built. I remarked to my friend who was fishing with me that it was rare to see a dipper leave water and fly above dry land. Well, on this October day, as we were rowing past the underground mouth of the burn, the dipper (for I imagine that it was the same bird, or at all events one of the same pair) again appeared and flew on the same course over the dry land. In October it could have had no nest, and I wondered what had caused it to fly up to this hill torrent where, it might have been thought, there was less food for it than in the loch or the river below. In June the rowans which grew beneath those splendid waterfalls were laden with snowy blossom; by the end of October the autumn storms had stripped them of all but a few of their soft red leaves, which harmonised with the richer crimson of the berries on which redwings were feeding. Salmon are heavy with spawn in Loch Dionard in October: we had gone there in the hopes of catching a late seatrout, which run in during October, though there are few of them.

Dippers are sometimes accused of eating the ova of salmon and trout. At the head of this loch, where a small river enters it in a series of shallow pools with a gravel bed, many salmon have their spawning grounds. That autumn (1942) the fish were unusually early in spawning, and by the last day of October the majority had shed their ova and had returned to the loch, where they would spend the winter before descending as kelts to the sea in early spring. My friend and I, after drawing up our boat on the shingle of the loch, walked up the river bank, expecting to find many fish still spawning, but most of them had finished these duties although the hollows which they had excavated in the gravel could be clearly seen. There must have been hundreds of thou-

The last Osprey's eyrie in Scotland.

From MacLeod's Table, looking across to the Cuillin,

sands of ova buried (some indeed imperfectly concealed) along that stretch of river, yet no dipper was to be seen, and I thought that this was a mark in the bird's favour. It may be of course that the dipper does on occasion feed on ova, but I am sure that the harm it does to the stock of salmon in a river is infinitesimal.

I happened to mention the early spawning of the salmon to one who has spent his long life as a salmon fisherman and deer stalker. He said at once that the reason for this was the high level of the river all summer and autumn, which enabled the fish to ascend quickly to the upper reaches. I accepted this explanation until I learned that on the Tweed also the spawning season of 1942 had been a record early one. Now the Tweed, unlike the Dionard, which is a river of the north west Highlands and thus receives almost continuous rain when the wind keeps (as it kept in 1942) persistently from the south west, is an east coast river. Tweed is indeed at its lowest during south westerly weather, and during the late summer and autumn of 1942 the river was not once in flood. But on Tweed also the salmon were spawning exceptionally early, and thus mere volume of water cannot, it seems, account for early spawning.

One of the most beautiful bird migrants to this country is the waxwing.[1] It does not visit us regularly, but there are certain seasons when it does appear in numbers. Such a season was 1941, when waxwings were reported from various parts of the Scottish Highlands. In the Isle of Skye that autumn I watched a party of five waxwings feeding on hawthorn berries. So far as I know, a waxwing had not been seen there since 1937. That year the birds visited Skye in late winter when the supply of berries had been exhausted, and I think that most of the waxwings died then of starvation. In 1941 my wife and I were travelling by car when we saw a strange bird on the road ahead of us. We stopped the car and watched the bird take wing and fly buoyantly to a thorn tree. As it flew the canary-coloured tip to the tail was conspicuous: when it perched the red 'sealing wax' spots on the wing secondaries, the black throat and the large feathery crest proclaimed it to be a waxwing. In the hawthorn tree were four more of the species; they fed greedily on the red berries, swallowing them whole and dropping carelessly to the ground more berries than they ate. In the midst of plenty, they had no thought for the morrow, but shared the feast with a number of black-

[1] The winter of 1943–4 saw another immigration of waxwings. There they remained until unusually late in the spring, and Frank Gordon, head stalker on the Balmoral forest, as late as April 8, 1944, watched a pair feeding on the berries of the cot on easter bushes on his cottage.

birds and one or two redwings. Waxwings usually are wandering birds, but when I passed the tree eight days later at least one of the party remained. It was gorged with berries and after a time flew idly to a branch where it remained almost motionless, breathing fast as though suffering from indigestion, its feathers puffed out, its eyes closed. For some minutes it rested thus, then suddenly returned to life and began to feed once more. Some of the berries it took as it hovered, warbler-like, in mid-air. It showed no fear of me, and although I was standing in the open on the road it flew deliberately towards me, and hovering in the air about eight feet from me, picked one berry after another from the tree.

About the time when I was watching the waxwings in Skye they were reported also from the Outer Hebrides, where they were seen on South Uist and on Barra.

During the last week of October, 1942, I was staying at a fishing lodge in the north west of Sutherland, in sight (on a clear day) of Skye to the south west, and Orkney to the north east. The lodge stands on a shoulder of a hill, six hundred feet above the sea. There are no trees in sight except a very small plantation of young trees, four to six feet high, round the house. On a previous visit in summer to the lodge I was interested to see a pair of very tame tree sparrows feeding a brood there, for the tree sparrow is now an uncommon bird in the Highlands of Scotland. The male can be identified by its chocolate (not bluish as in the house sparrow) head and the white patch on either cheek. It is less cheeky and aggressive than the house sparrow, a bird which I wish might be banished from the Highlands, where it thrives even in the stormiest and most wind-swept places.

On this visit I saw no tree sparrow, but when the wind turned to the north east and blew persistently from that quarter for a week a number of interesting migrants visited the plantation, the hillside near it, and the river in the strath below. These birds had crossed the sea from Scandinavia, and when they first arrived were weary and reluctant to take wing when disturbed. On the short grass, out on the bare hillside, chaffinches fed: their food must have been different to their usual woodland diet in Scandinavian forests. Bramblings haunted the heather. Like the chaffinches, whose near relation they are, they went singly. On the ground the brambling might be mistaken for a chaffinch, but immediately it takes flight the flash of white at the base of the tail is characteristic. The brambling nests in the birch woods which grow round Tromsö in the north of Norway; the nests I saw there were not high in the trees.

One day a flock of grey geese, flying high in formation, passed up the strath where I was fishing. They were moving fast toward the south, and when last I saw them were approaching the head of the strath and the storm clouds that hung low upon the hills over which it was necessary for them to pass.

But the most lovely sight of that week was a skein of snow-white whooper swans which were travelling, curiously enough, against the wind and toward the north east. The summer home of the whooper is Iceland, which land lies north west of the Scottish Highlands. I think it probable that the north wind which prevailed during their long overseas flight had carried the whoopers farther south than they intended before they made their landfall on the Scottish coast, and it was therefore necessary for them to fly back up the coast to the loch which is their winter quarters. They were moving slowly, and seemed tired, as they might well have been, for the coast of Sutherland is 600 miles from Iceland.

I doubt whether whoopers alight on the sea during their migration flight. Unless the sea were calm (an unlikely event at that season of the year) they would find it very unpleasant, for they are not, like true seabirds, used to breaking waves and could not dive through them like guillemots or little auks. If whooper swans do alight on salt water—and this they do rarely—they choose a sheltered bay, with an off-shore wind and calm water. From October until April, and sometimes until early May, certain Highland fresh-water lochs have a steady whooper population. Should a prolonged spell of frost freeze the waters of these lochs the swans betake themselves to the rivers. They are sometimes seen on the upper Spey, but in the rivers the water weeds on which they feed are not plentiful and at the first opportunity the swans return to the lochs.

There was one migrant which I saw during this period of autumn movement in an unexpected place. It was a long-tailed duck, or I should say drake, for he was a male of the species. He was diving for food eagerly in the peaty waters of a hill loch, and until I had watched him carefully through my stalking glass I was doubtful of his identity. Long-tailed duck are regular autumn and winter visitors to the Scottish coast, but this is the first time I had seen one feeding, or resting, on a fresh-water loch inland. It is perhaps strange that this should be so, for in its Icelandic haunts this duck nests on islands of fresh-water lakes and is not, like the eider, a frequenter of salt-water lochs in summer.

The long-tailed drake in winter plumage is a handsome fellow. His head and flanks are mainly white and the rest of his plumage white mixed with dark brown. His long and pointed tail is often trailed in the water, but when the bird is eager or excited is held jauntily in the air. In Europe the long-tailed duck breeds plentifully on Lake Myvatn in northern Iceland, where I saw the eggs in thick undergrowth on an island and a large brood of young on a tarn on the crown of the same island. Other European breeding sites are in Spitsbergen (where the species is not plentiful although I saw one nest near the shore of Ice Fjord), on Bear Island, in Norway, Sweden, Finland and Russia. In Britain a nest was reported from one of the Orkney Islands in 1911 and again in 1912.

In the season of 1943 that rare bird the Hoopoe visited Strath Dionard. George Ross, stalker at Gualann, a keen naturalist and observer, had a close view of this unusual visitor. It was a fine calm day of late autumn, unusually mild for the time of the year. The river and the tributary burns ran low, and he had gone up the strath to see the salmon at the spawning beds. Ahead of him from the heather rose a strange brightly plumaged bird with butterfly-like flight and large crest. It was apparently very tired and allowed a near approach, raising and depressing its crest as the observer stood watching it. On returning home and consulting one of his bird books, George Ross had no difficulty in identifying the stranger as a hoopoe. The inconsequent flight, the long curved bill, the pinkish plumage, with boldly barred wings and back, were unmistakable. The crest feathers were tipped with black; the tail was black, white at the base.

As might be inferred from its bright colouring the hoopoe is most numerous in more southerly latitudes than Scotland. It has occasionally nested in the south counties of England. In North West Africa and West Asia it is not uncommon as a nesting species. From Italy it nests northward through Europe to Southern Sweden and Poland. It winters in tropical Africa, Arabia, and South India. That Sutherland migrant may have been on passage to its winter haunts from Sweden and have been blown on a south easterly wind drift across the North Sea. The next day George Ross returned to Strath Dionard, but the rare visitor was not to be found; it was then perhaps winging its way toward the south, from the autumnal mist and gloom of the north west Highlands to the warmth and sunshine of Africa and Arabia.

Thus far in this chapter I have written mainly on birds, but no description of the Highlands in October would be complete without a reference to the rutting and roaring of that antlered king of many a Highland glen—the red deer. Much of the Highlands is deer forest land. This latest world war sees the Highland deer forests passing through critical days. Even before the war the value of the forests was declining, for the modern shooting tenant, less anxious to endure hardships than his predecessors, preferred grouse shooting to deer-stalking.

Now sheep and Highland cattle pasture on many of the forests, but in some Highland forests no animal except the red deer could live.

In October is the mating season of the deer. At dusk on an October night when walking through a lonely glen I have heard the crack of antler against antler as two stags rushed upon one another. The fight is usually broken off before much damage has been done, but I have heard of instances when the vanquished beast has been found dead or dying, with deep wounds in his body. Scrope mentions a particularly savage conflict that was fatal to both stags. 'Two large harts' he writes 'after a furious and deadly thrust, had entangled their horns so firmly together that they were inextricable, and the victor remained with the vanquished. In this situation they were discovered by the forester, who killed the survivor, whilst he was yet struggling to release himself from his dead antagonist. The horns remain at Gordon Castle, still locked together as they were found.'

Through the October day, and also throughout the October night, the hoarse challenge of stag to stag echoes through many a Highland glen and pass. Sometimes deep, sometimes cracked and hoarse, are these voices. The unseen rivals listen for the reply to a challenge, and after roaring run a little way in the direction of the answering cry. When they come in sight of one another the speed of the advance is accelerated, or perhaps one of the animals, not liking the looks of his opponent, gives ground slowly, and with what dignity he can muster.

It is not difficult to mimic a stag's roar, or to draw an answering roar in reply. I have often brought a beast near to me, but usually the stag becomes suspicious when yet he is some hundreds of yards away, hesitates and then sheers off, or else circles round to get the 'wind' of the object of his suspicions. When he has got one's 'wind', that is the end of the whole business, for when he scents his enemy, man, this spells danger to him with a big D, and he takes precipitate flight. The roar of a hill stag brings back to my mind autumn days of long ago on the hill —days when the mist swept low across Carn a' Mhaim, and spread an impenetrable curtain over Ben MacDhui and Braeriach; when the moon, breaking through the cloud and shining on Glen Lui, bathed the strong branches of those old pines which are unchanging with the years and seem everlasting as the hills themselves. For a time there would be silence and then, out of the mist cap, would come the hoarse challenge from an invisible stag, and perhaps the dark antlered form of his rival would be seen as he crossed the path ahead, his hinds respectfully following him.

Stags rarely have to use their gift of swimming, yet they can if necessary swim far and well. They have been seen more than once swimming the tide-swept strait which separates the Isle of Mull from the mainland of Morvern. That icy strait is a couple of miles wide and so they should find no difficulty in crossing the sea from the Isle of Skye to the mainland, for here the passage is less than a mile from shore to shore.

I end this chapter with a brief description of a remarkable migration of Swallows to Shetland in October 1942. A correspondent, who was then stationed on one of these northern isles, tells me that swallows invaded the whole archipelago. He says there must have been hundreds, even thousands of these birds; they were in each glen and valley, and remained for several days. In Shetland the swallow is a rare bird, and these must have been migrants from Scandinavia. He said that it was a great joy to see so many of the swallows, especially so late in the season when the Highland swallows had long ago left for the south. The appearance of the birds in such numbers is all the more remarkable because the year 1942 was a bad swallow season throughout the British Isles, and in all districts a marked scarcity of nesting birds was recorded.

torms may uninterruptedly travel across the Highlands in November, but there are years when the month is calm and peaceful. There is a soft quality in the November light: that is due partly to the low sun which each morning further delays his rising and even at noon fails to mount above the higher hills, now carrying their first coating of winter snow.

It is one of the charms of a November day that unexpected legacies of summer are sometimes seen in unexpected places. One day early in that month I climbed Foinne Bheinn, the highest hill of the Reay Forest in North West Sutherland—and here I ought perhaps to say that there are Highland deer forests in which no tree grows, or can even be seen from their high ground. My way on this hill climb had taken me first along the banks of the salmon-haunted Dionard river, where the dark shapes of fish could be seen in the amber-tinted pools. When I reached Dugal's Pool I left the river, and climbed to Dugal's Corrie, where lies Dugal's Loch. I wondered then, as I have sometimes wondered since, who was this Dugal, for his name remains long after all record of him has been lost. Was he a skilled angler, and did the corrie take its name from the pool where he landed many a silvery salmon, fresh-run from the green sea depths, or was he a celebrated deerstalker and hunter so that the corrie from some hunting exploit was named after him and the pool took its name from the corrie above it? In the Reay Country, which received its name from Lord Reay their chief, the MacKays were for long the leading family. There is an old Pibroch—a Pibroch is a composition of classical bagpipe music—with the name Lament for Donald Dugal MacKay, a lovely tune with an especial sweetness in it. That, at all events, is the popular name for the tune, but a distinguished Celtic scholar told me that the correct name should in fact be Donald Duachal, the word Duachal, which is old Gaelic, signifying Dauntless— a fine term to be applied to any man.

After this short digression let me return to Dugal's Corrie, above which the radiant peak of Foinne Bheinn in virgin snow rose against the blue of the sky. In the corrie the grass was brown, the heather bloom long since withered, and the sodden ground newly imprisoned beneath a crust of frost, yet a single scabious flower, large and deep blue, rose from these sere acres and gave me, as it seemed, a message of summer days when the sun was warm, the air heather-scented and the grass of the corrie soft and green. A flower, unexpectedly seen, sometimes brings back to me the memory of my mother. She, like the mother of W. H. Hudson, loved flowers, for she had, in an unusual degree, a love for all that was beautiful. During my early wanderings, if I came upon a wild rose with a specially fragrant scent, or a spray of bell heather of an unusually lovely red, I used sometimes to take those flowers home to her, for I knew that they would bring her joy. In his *Far Away and Long Ago* Hudson describes his mother and her love for beautiful things in the delicate prose of which he was a master.

But with the passing of the years I am inclined to leave a flower on its stalk, although I often stoop down to breathe in the fragrance of a wild rose, or a scented orchis, or the honey scent of a clustered head of the rosy moss campion, opening its hardy flowers close to the blinding glare from some snowfield of the high Cairngorms or of the tundra of Iceland. The most exquisite pictures of flowers photographed on and stored by the mind are the blossoms that grew, free as the air they breathed, and not gathered into a vase within the confines of a room. In his poem *Forbearance*, Ralph Waldo Emerson puts things very well:

> *Hast thou named all the birds without a gun?*
> *Loved the wood-rose, and left it on its stalk?*
> *At rich men's tables eaten bread and pulse?*
> *Unarmed, faced danger with a heart of trust?*
> *And loved so well a high behaviour,*
> *In man or maid, that thou from speech refrained,*
> *Nobility more nobly to repay?*
> *O, be my friend, and teach me to be thine!*

Emerson in one of his essays recalls that the ancients called beauty the flowering of virtue. In some of these essays that great author seems to have come very near to the heart of beauty. But was he right when he wrote:

'Flowers so strictly belong to youth, that we adult men soon come to feel that their beautiful generations concern not us: we have had our day; now let the children have theirs. The flowers jilt us, and we are old bachelors with their ridiculous tenderness'?

It seems to me that, with some of us at least, our love of flowers continues unchanged, and even intensified, with the passing years: that the beauty of a flower, a bird, a cloud, sunset and sunrise, evoke in us the same response in later, more anxious years as in the fullness of youth.

When I had climbed through Dugal's Corrie to the ridge of Foinne Bheinn I saw ahead of me a young stag feeding, then lost sight of him. When I reached the ridge the young animal received the fright of its life, for I suddenly appeared beside him as he rested, chewing the cud, on a grassy sun-warmed bank.

Beyond the ridge the snow was continuous; on it were the tracks of fox and hare and, more unexpected, the footprints of an otter. The ridge lay between the two salmon rivers, Laxford and Dionard, and the otter had perhaps crossed the high pass of Foinne Bheinn from the rocky pools of the Laxford and as an expert fisherman was hoping to try his luck in the Dionard. Otters in a river pool strike terror into the hearts of the salmon inhabiting it, for they know that this land animal is their master even in their native element. One day a friend and I were walking beside the river Feshie not far from its source amongst the Cairngorms. On the banks of a pool we found a freshly killed salmon, untouched except for a bite taken out of the shoulder—that part of the salmon which is the otter's favourite cut. My friend took the fish home with him, and it provided him with supper and breakfast for several days. It is strange that the otter should eat only that shoulder cut: at the beginning of the present war the human consumer paid 20/- per lb. for any cut of a salmon.

Near the otter's tracks on the snow of Foinne Bheinn a ptarmigan rose on white wings and disappeared over the ridge into the corrie. Alas, before we could reach the hilltop the mist swept in on the north west wind. Fog-crystals in beautiful fern-shape grew from the rocks: the frozen moisture in the fog fell as delicate spicules of ice. Here, at three thousand feet above the sea, the frost was sufficient to freeze the water vapour in the air. To freeze the spray of the waves—a sight never witnessed in Scotland—an immeasurably more severe frost is necessary. A friend of mine, the captain of one of His Majesty's Ships, told me that when on escort duties with a convoy bound for Murmansk the spray from the great waves that broke over his vessel reached the bridge as ice—the spray froze in less than three seconds when suspended in that bitter air.

Behind the cairn that marks the highest point of Foinne Bheinn I waited in a mist-filled land. From time to time for a few brief seconds black cliffs showed, then were blotted out again in the grey, blue-tinted cloak of mist. Although during these periods the gloom lightened and the blue of the sky showed overhead the hilltop remained for the rest of that short November day hidden in cloud and when on my descent I had at length passed beyond the zone of cloud I could see that the hills to the east—Ben Hope, Ben Loyal and Morven—were, each one of them, shrouded in a white mist cap.

That day I saw no eagle—when I write of the eagle I mean the golden eagle, for that is the only eagle now left to us in Scotland—nor even a buzzard. The buzzard, a noble enough bird in the air but of a meaner fibre than the eagle when seen at close quarters, is a fowl of the lower moors rather than the high tops. Of recent years it has established itself on some of the Outer Hebrides where is (or was) the haunt of the hen harrier, and is said to be responsible for the decrease of that beautiful and graceful harrier. It is certainly true that buzzard and harrier are rarely found living near one another.

A habit—I think it is a comparatively recent habit—which the buzzard has acquired is to perch motionless for hours upon a telegraph pole. So tame—or lethargic—is the great bird that a passing train or motor car fails to induce it to move from its perch, on which it is, although apparently half asleep, doubtless keeping a sharp look-out for any rat, mouse or rabbit moving in its field of vision. I have yet to see an eagle on a telegraph post, although, as I shall narrate in a subsequent chapter, this was once reported to me.

By November one might have thought that the last of the summer migrants would have left the Highlands but from time to time belated swallows, and occasionally even swifts, are seen. On November 11, 1923, my wife and I watched for some time a pair of swifts wheeling above the leafless birches at Aviemore, in central Inverness-shire. The Cairngorms at the time were deeply snow-covered, but the day was mild and the wind from the south west. When it is remembered that the Scottish swifts leave the country for the south in August, while full summer remains with us, that November record for a district in the heart of the Highlands is a remarkable one. It is generally presumed that those birds must have been on passage from the far North, perhaps from Norway, where the nesting season of the swift is later than in this country and where the birds are still rearing their young in August. But surely the weather in Norway in early November or even October would fail to provide a livelihood for an insect-eating bird like the swift? Early naturalists were insistent that birds hibernated, and I think that they would have taken this appearance of a pair of swifts in November—especially as the day was the first mild one after a cold spell—as evidence to support their belief. It all hangs on what we understand by the term hibernation. It has been found that swifts do indeed become torpid when a cold spell with snow visits the Highlands after these birds of glorious flight have arrived at their nesting haunts. The insect life on which they feed entirely disappears during these cold spells, and swifts at such times have been found huddling in a moribund state in the holes under the eaves of the houses where they nest. If it is necessary for the swift to do this in May, when the sun at noon is high in the heavens, it must surely be equally necessary during frost and snow in early November. Therefore that pair of swifts, seen under a grey November sky, present a baffling problem. Can they have been hibernating (I use this

24

word for the want of a better) from time to time during their journey
south and taking advantage of milder hours to snatch a few billfuls of
insects, and if so were they able to reach a sufficiently southerly latitude
before winter in real earnest set in? If not, they must have hibernated
in very truth or else perished.

Swifts, in Britain at all events, are most regular in leaving us during
the first fortnight of August. But in the summer of 1942 they delayed
their departure. A friend in Edinburgh tells me that they were later in
leaving that district than he ever remembered; it was not until August
25 that they vanished, and the same late departure was chronicled from
other districts. That a delay of even a fortnight should be reckoned
noteworthy in their departure is a striking commentary on the strange-
ness of those November swifts.

Recently I made a journey by air across the Scottish Highlands from
Inverness to Orkney. From ground level at Inverness Loch Ness is
invisible, but when we had climbed a few hundred feet into the air and
were swinging round preparatory to setting our course north for the
hundred and fifteen mile journey which lay between us and Orkney,
the loch, set in its theatre of mist-wreathed hills, could be seen stretch-
ing away in beauty toward the west. Loch Ness, one of the deepest
lochs of the Highlands—Loch Morar on the Atlantic seaboard of Inverness county is actually the deepest—will, I suppose be celebrated to
future generations as the home of that strange creature the Loch Ness
Monster. The first reports of this creature were greeted with unbelief,
even with derision, but since those days it has been watched by so many
trustworthy witnesses, some of them personally known to me, that I
am unable to believe it to be a mere product of the imagination.
During the last decade the Loch Ness monster has been frequently seen,
but its appearances date much further back than that. I know of elderly
persons living near Loch Ness who as children were frightened by their
nurses, who warned them that they would be taken by the beast of
Loch Ness if they were naughty. A year or two before the first World
War began in 1914 a certain respected resident of the Loch Ness
district was one summer day rowing down the loch. When he landed he
was obviously upset, but when questioned as to the reason for his
shaken nerves he was at first evasive in his replies. At last he said 'I do
not expect you to believe me, but this is my story: As I was rowing
down the loch just now a beast came to the surface of the water not far
from me. All I want to say about it is that I never wish to see the like of
it again.' More recently the Monster has been seen by Mr. Goodbody
of Invergarry House and his daughter, who watched it carefully through

a stalking telescope for at least forty minutes, and by a friend of mine Mr. C. B. Farrell.

Mr. C. B. Farrell while on duty with the Royal Observer Corps at 5.15 a.m. Greenwich Time on the morning of May 25th, 1943, saw a strange object on Loch Ness.

When he looked at the object through his binoculars he saw a creature twenty-five to thirty feet long at a distance of 250 yards from him. In colour the creature was dark olive above and cygnet brown on the flanks. The thing which chiefly impressed the observer was the size of the eyes, which were very prominent. The neck was graceful and about four feet long, and at the back of the neck was a curious fin. The Monster was apparently feeding. Slowly and gracefully it depressed head and neck before they were submerged, and a few seconds later quickly withdrew them from the water, vigorously shook its head, and at once submerged it again. Through his Zeiss X6 binoculars each movement of the Monster was clear.

Mr. Farrell told me that the most remarkable thing was the manner in which the Monster finally disappeared. There was no diving, nor any splash: the whole body subsided vertically without a ripple.

Father Cyril Dieckhoff, O.S.B. has kept full notes in his diary of the various appearances of the Loch Ness Monster, and he has very kindly sent me these notes, and has given me permission to use them in this book.

He begins by pointing out an interesting and little-known fact—that the 'Monsters' which inhabited the three large and deep Highland lochs, Ness, Shiel and Morar, were so well known by the old Gaelic-speaking people that they had distinctive names. The Loch Ness Monster was spoken of as *An Niseag*, the Loch Shiel Monster as *An Seileag*, and the Loch Morar Monster as *A' Mhorag*. Father Cyril describes his talks with some of the old people of the Moidart district, who were a singularly fine type of Highlander—upright and intelligent, and close observers of nature. Their evidence agrees in describing the humps which are a feature of the Loch Ness Monster. One observer said that when the head (which resembled a horse's head) disappeared a big hump (cnàp mór) emerged instead.

The appearances of the Loch Shiel and Loch Morar Monsters are few compared with those of the Loch Ness Monster, but this is only to be expected, for both Loch Shiel and Loch Morar are very lonely lochs compared with Loch Ness.

Father Cyril has twice seen the Loch Ness Monster, although on neither occasion was the creature exposed sufficiently for him to give an accurate description of it, but various members of the community of the Fort Augustus monastery have been more fortunate.

Brother Richard Horan on May 26, 1934, was working at a pump near the Abbey Boathouse when he heard a noise coming from the loch. At first he paid no attention to the noise for he thought it was caused by a herring drifter on passage through the loch. After a time, happening to look up, he saw a large creature near the canal pier. It was no more than thirty yards from him, and was swimming parallel to the shore of the loch opposite the Abbey grounds. The beast had its head turned towards him. The head was not unlike that of a seal but very small, and the head and neck had a most graceful appearance. A broad, whitish stripe was visible running down the front of the neck. He noticed a curious motion of the water behind the animal as though a propeller was working. For some time Brother Horan watched the strange visitor, until it plunged beneath the surface, causing a great commotion in the loch. After its disappearance its track, closely resembling the track of a torpedo, was clearly visible proceeding in a north-easterly direction.

The Dutch scientist Count G. A. Bentinck visited Loch Ness in the summer of 1935 and again in 1936 to make observations on the Loch Ness Monster. Count Bentinck records his observations in the Dutch periodical *De levende Natuur* (W. Versluys, Amsterdam (O) Jaargagg 40, ctfl 7). The article is entitled 'Het Dier van Loch Ness'. Count Bentinck's first observation of the creature was from the Half Way House on the shore of Loch Ness on August 10, 1935. He saw through his field glasses a hump rising from the loch in the direction of Foyers, in shape and size like an upturned rowing boat. Two days later he saw exactly the same thing. Ten days of rough weather from the south west ensued and prevented further observations, but on August 24, a fine, calm morning, when he looked out of his bedroom window at 7.30 a.m., he saw in the little bay below the house the top of the creature's head rising above the loch's surface, and from it a kind of steam came forth, but was blown back by a slight cold breeze. It was, writes the Count, undoubtedly the warm, moist breath of a mammal. A passing car alarmed the creature, which sank, but half an hour later returned and remained on the surface, keeping its position until the wash of a passing steamer reached it, when it submerged. Count Bentinck, who left the district with no doubt of the existence of the strange animal, concludes his article with the following Latin lines:

'Nolite existimare omnia animalia, in primis marina, nota esse.
Vivere sola quae ipse norit, quis-quis arbitratur, stultus est.'

The Loch Ness Monster is usually spoken of in the singular, but if indeed it does exist the probability is that it is not alone. At least one

observer is confident that he has seen two 'Monsters' making a commotion at the same time in different parts of Loch Ness, and two boys
from the Abbey school at Fort Augustus were positive that they had
seen several young of the species.

Towards the end of June, 1937, they were returning in a boat to the
Abbey when, on looking down into the water from the stern, they
observed three small creatures swimming away from the wash. Father
Cyril interviewed the lads and obtained from them a detailed description of the creatures. The beasts resembled large lizards, and were
about three feet in length. They had two pairs of rudimentary legs and
a tail 7 or 8 inches long. Each pair of legs was used for swimming, but
the motion of each pair was different; the forelegs had a waving motion
and the hind legs were used to push the animals forward. The skin was
dark grey and a distinct neck was visible.

The following month Professor Diverres of Swansea gave Father
Cyril a detailed description of the Monster, which he had seen that day,
and of which he had drawn, on the spot, a convincing sketch in ink,
showing the characteristic humps.

Captain Grant, master of MacBrayne's steamer *Gondolier*, which in
summer regularly plied from one end of Loch Ness to the other before
the outbreak of war in 1939, told me that he had twice seen the
Monster, and each time at a distance. He was convinced that it was a
shy creature, and that the noise of the steamer paddles alarmed it;
indeed most of the people who have seen and watched it have remarked
on its shyness. Most of the witnesses agree that the neck is long and
slender and that the body rarely appears above the water's surface. It is
usually seen in comparatively shallow water. Why, it may be asked, is
the Loch Ness monster now reported so frequently as compared to, let
us say, twenty years ago? The explanation is simple. The old road along
the loch was screened from the water by trees: the modern highway
has an almost uninterrupted outlook over the water. The appearances
were apparently more numerous when the new road was being made
along the shore of the loch and it is possible that the great masses of
rock blasted beside and sometimes actually into the loch may have
made the monster nervous and restless. Then, again, it must be remembered that the creature is now as it were common property, but
formerly those who saw it hesitated to talk of what they had seen, for
fear of ridicule, or even worse.

I believe the Loch Ness Monster to be a species of Large Pinni-
pede which formerly inhabited several, perhaps many, of the large
fresh-water lochs of the Highlands. Hear what the Earl of Malmesbury,
who was then tenant of Lochiel's forest of Achnacarry at the time,

writes in his *Memoirs* in the year 1857, of the strange water creature then inhabiting Loch Arkaig:

'My stalker, John Stuart at Achnacarry, has seen it twice and both times at sunrise in summer, when there was not a ripple on the water. The creature was basking on the surface; he saw only the head and hind-quarters, proving that its back was hollow, which is not the shape of any fish, or of a seal. Its head resembled that of a horse. The Highlanders are very superstitious about this creature. They believe that there is never more than one in existence at the same time.'

It is interesting to note that a number of persons who have seen the Monster of Loch Ness have described its head as resembling that of a horse.

Loch Morar, deepest of Scottish fresh-water lochs—its bed, where twilight reigns at noon, is 1080 feet below the surface—has, as I have mentioned, its Monster. Loch Ness is 754 feet deep; Loch Morar, according to Sir Archibald Geikie, is the deepest known hollow on any part of the European plateau, with the exception of the submarine valley which skirts the southern part of Scandinavia, and is indeed deeper than any part of the Atlantic for at least 100 miles to the west of it. The Monster of Loch Morar was believed to appear before the death of a MacDonald of Morar.

With this digression on the Loch Ness Monster let me return to my flight north from Inverness. We passed high over the Black Isle, where is one of the few inland colonies in Britain of the fulmar petrel, and above the stately castle of Dunrobin which stands beside the sea, and saw ahead of us the cone of Morven in Caithness, one of the most distinctive of Scottish hills. As we passed high above that heather-clad cone I recalled that the eagle formerly nested here and that an osprey made its home on the river beneath the hill for some weeks during the autumn of 1934.

Very soon we were over the Pentland Firth and saw ahead of us the 1000-feet sheer cliff which forms the western side of Hoy, the High Island, most southerly of the Orkney group. As we skirted those grim cliffs I was interested to see fulmars sailing with their unmistakable flight backwards and forwards near the summit of the precipice. On my return journey three days later, when the wind was stronger and the great Atlantic waves were breaking with prodigious force into the sea caves beneath that high precipice, the fulmars were still there, revelling in the storm. The fulmars of the Isle of Skye and, so far as I know, of all the breeding stations on the Scottish mainland, leave the cliffs at the end of the nesting season and are not seen again until after the New Year, yet I am informed that the cliffs of Hoy are never at any time during the winter months without their fulmar population.

During this visit to Orkney at the end of November I had an opportunity of visiting the island of South Ronaldshay, a wind-swept isle which ends in a low promontory beside the Pentland Firth. On those low rocky shores I saw several flocks of snow buntings. These small white-winged birds, of the size of a lark, are visitors from the far north—from Greenland, Iceland and Spitsbergen. They have two distinct winter haunts in Scotland; the lonely shores of coast and island, and the high hills. On the coast their food is the seeds of the sea plantain, bent, or grass; on the high hills the seeds of grasses and perhaps the catkins of the prostrate alpine willow. Among each flock of snow buntings are usually one or two cocks in the handsome black and white plumage of the breeding season. The cry is a tinkling whistle. Larks haunted the grassy tussocks beside the shore. Many larks at the approach of winter arrive at the islands of the Orkney and Shetland groups and of the Hebrides, and it has been proved that individuals from far distant Siberia come to us. Sometimes in the half light of a winter's morning I have flushed a skylark from the tussock where it has slept during the long winter night. With a flash of white from its under plumage it has risen at my feet and flown snipe-like away, to disappear at once into the dawn. I like to think on a November night of wind and storm, of many larks, each snug behind his or her tussock, sleeping warm and dry while, a few inches above them, the storm rages and the lances of the hail torment the shuddering earth. Tussocks of grass provide shelter not only for larks—snipe and woodcock use them, and hares shelter behind, or in them.

On South Ronaldshay are farms of considerable size and when I was near the south shore I watched feeding towards me across a field of stubble one of the largest flocks of rock pigeons I have seen. Although it was the end of November the harvest had only now been secured and the rock doves—there were many scores of them—were eagerly feeding on the grain left among the stubble. As the flock fed quickly forward the birds in the rear were almost continuously rising and flying over the backs of their fellows to take their places in the front line, so the scene was one of intense activity, fascinating to watch. I remained without movement and the flock passed close to me, so that I could see the iridescent green feathers of the necks and the beautiful blue-grey plumage of the backs. The rock dove still breeds plentifully in the sea cliffs of Scotland,[1] but so far as is known the pure wild type is found no longer on the coasts of England and Wales.

[1] I have seen one small inland colony in the Isle of Skye.

The new edition of the *Handbook of British Birds*, which stands supreme at the present day among modern British ornithological works, mentions that in many parts of the coasts of Wales and England feral domestic pigeons breed and that on the Yorkshire coast a mixture of wild and feral types occur, with the wild type predominating. The peregrine falcon preys on the wild rock pigeon. On one occasion I looked out of my window in the Isle of Skye and saw standing on the gravel beneath it what at first I thought must be a tame pigeon, for the bird on seeing me did not attempt to fly away, but remained quietly on the ground. Then I saw that a large female peregrine falcon was 'waiting' overhead.

When I went out the rock dove hurried into a ditch for cover and although the falcon flew over it and endeavoured to make her quarry rise, the pigeon sat tight, and after a time she flew off to hunt elsewhere.

In Skye the rock doves are seen usually in small flocks, but on this Orkney island of South Ronaldshay they are evidently more numerous. Later that afternoon I saw their enemy the peregrine. He—for by his small size the bird must have been a male—had been standing on the top of a cliff, and when he saw me sailed along the cliff, then gradually descended over the sea to a lower level. But here the wind was gusty and variable and there were down draughts and air pockets which gave trouble even to so skilled a flier as a peregrine. No longer could he soar or fly swiftly and evenly as is his wont; he was obliged to drive his wings at their utmost speed in order to retain his height and avoid being pressed down to the waves.

Before sunset a strong wind arose out of the north west and snow flurries swept the isles of Orkney: it was then strange to see, within three days of the coming of December, a horse reaper making a start at cutting a field of oats, beaten down by storms and with much of the grain already lost.

The old Celtic name for Orkney was Orcaib, from the word Orc, a young boar. It was a tribal name, as was also Cataibh, from the word Cat, the old name for Sutherland.

In Skye the raven is not uncommon. We see him almost daily. Some years ago one of our hens took to laying beneath a straggling whin bush. One of a pair of ravens which were nesting in a sea cliff about a mile from our house got to know of this hen's nesting place. He even seemed to know when the hen would lay, and scarcely had she deposited her egg when the raven would fly over, drop down to the whin bush, seize the egg in his bill, and fly away with it in triumph, perhaps to feed his sitting mate. One November afternoon a friend and I were on Rudha Hunish in Skye. We were looking out over the cliff to the dark waters of the Minch where, midway between Skye and Harris, the island group of Fladday Chuain rose against the darkening sky. Earlier in the autumn gannets would have been fishing in the bay beneath us, but a common gull and a few shags were all that we now saw. Then round a headland a raven suddenly flew into our view. The bird had his legs stretched earthward as though he had been about to alight—as perhaps he had when his keen eye had seen us and he had continued his flight. But a little later he returned with his mate and gave us an exhibition of the upside-down flying which all ravens love. The sudden turning of a raven on his back to fly upside-down, or rather to *soar* in that strange position for a few brief seconds, is an evolution carried out so swiftly that the human eye cannot follow it, and we shall have to await a slow-motion film of the process to tell us how it is done. My own impression is that the turn is made from the right. Equally swift is the righting of the bird; the whole is one continuous glide and when the reversal of the position is made there is no checking of the speed. So far as I know, the raven is unique among British birds in flying or gliding upside-down. I think that both male and female raven do this. The act is, I am sure, one of sheer abandon; it takes place usually when the bird is a considerable distance above the ground and often when the raven has flown a little way out to sea from a high cliff.

On this occasion I had with me Dara, our black and tan collie. Dara is the second of two collies my wife and I have owned. Dara is an unusual dog, very friendly and intelligent and a grand companion. She loves swimming, and when she accompanies me on a walk across the hills to a distant loch in which I sometimes fish she knows each peaty pool on the moor. She goes far ahead of me, so that I think for a time that she is lost, but when I reach the pool I find her standing there expectantly, awaiting my arrival for the slight encouragement needed for her to spring in and swim around. Her greatest delight is to paw the bottom of these pools, and to force bubbles of marsh gas to the surface: these she endeavours to catch, talking excitedly to herself all the time. If a stick be thrown to her she likes nothing better than to spring from a high bank into the pool, disappearing entirely beneath the surface and on coming again to the top of the water seizing the stick and swimming in triumph to the shore. If the bank is too steep for her to climb out she does not, like some dogs, lose her head; she calmly sets about looking for some place where she *can* climb on to dry land. Until two winters ago I used to bathe in the sea before breakfast all the year round. There is a natural bathing pool with about fifteen feet of water in it at high tide below our house and of a frosty

Young grey seal, about eight weeks old, swimming in a rock-pool on its island.

Cow Atlantic Seal.

winter's morning it was sometimes Dara and sometimes I who took that first icy plunge. Those were cold swims in the half-light when all the earth to the tide mark was frozen iron-hard and when there was ice even on the rock pools where the sea anemones were torpid from the cold, but the splendour of the rising sun upon the snow-clad hills of the Outer Hebrides on our return journey was an ample reward for that cold walk and swim. Sometimes in rough winter weather one had to time to a nicety one's plunge into the pool so as to be able to climb out during a momentary lessening in the fury of the waves. Dara, I have discovered, watches the far-out oncoming waves just as carefully as I do and if she sees a distant wave of unusual size, even a considerable time before it has approached the shore and broken, she cannot be induced to enter the water. She has learned, from long association with me, to take an interest in the birds she sees. There is a certain walk we take which brings us near a golden eagle's eyrie and I have seen Dara watching the eagle intently as it sailed backwards and forwards above the cliff. She is usually well-disposed toward birds but once when she had puppies and a raven flew low over a neighbouring field she gave hot chase and appeared to be very angry indeed. One day during a walk Dara sprained or strained one foreleg and was limping ahead of me when Meg, my eldest daughter's Border terrier and a great friend of Dara's, ran up to her, wagging her tail and in the plainest possible manner expressing her sympathy. The incident was a charming one. Telepathy between two persons is, I believe, a more frequent event than is generally realised: telepathy between a human being and a dog is rarer. On one occasion at least I was in touch with Dara at a distance. I was on a visit to another part of the Highlands and she was not with me. I had been on the high hills and was descending into a warm sunny corrie, perfumed by crowberry and hill grasses, when I had a vision of her at home watching for me outside the house. Those who have had the experience of being in touch at a distance with a kindred soul—my wife and I have often had that experience—will understand me when I say that the experience is impressed upon the mind in a clear, unmistakable manner and the whole scene where one happened to be at the time is engraved distinctly. I can now recall the corrie, the deerstalker and his collie dog as though I was again living that moment, and I believe that the deerstalker's collie acted as an unconscious medium between me and Dara. Axel Munthe, in his celebrated book *San Michele*, records that he has been in touch telepathically with one of his dogs.

This short discourse on what may be termed the occult has put me in mind of the remarkable behaviour of a pony—a Shetland pony with Arab blood in her—named Pinto which we had when our children were small. The family were in the habit of going for expeditions in a small pony cart which they called the Pinto cart. They were returning one afternoon with their governess and when they had reached a part of the road where it winds along the sea coast beneath cliffs and a steep hill face covered with screes and large boulders the pony came to a halt. Nothing would induce it to move forward, and in the end the occupants of the pony cart were obliged to alight and by dint of much pushing and pulling by the united family the pony was forced to progress a few yards, when all at once it was eager and anxious to trot homeward once more. About four hours later, my wife and I were motoring along the road, and found that a huge boulder had fallen from the cliff, and had come to rest on the road. When we reached home we heard the story of Pinto's strange behaviour, and saw later that where she had come to a halt and had stood trembling and obviously upset was the place where the boulder subsequently fell. Had she second sight, or did she sense the vibrations of the boulder which it perhaps made some hours before it actually fell?

When she was a child of ten our second daughter, Bride, was riding Smoky, Pinto's foal. At a bend of the road, where it crosses a lonely part of the moor, she saw a person lying wounded on the ground. She dismounted to help him, but before she reached the spot the figure dissolved in air. Was she seeing back into some clan fight of the past? Near the place was a loch, named Lochan nan Ceann, the Loch of the Heads. The loch has now been drained, but it is said that long ago a bitter fight was waged between the MacLeods and the MacDonalds there. In those days there was a large loch, named Loch Chaluim Chille, at Kilmuir, and on an island of the loch stood a monastery, the ruins of which remain to this day. MacDonald of the Isles had fallen out with the abbot of this monastery, and had prevailed upon MacLeod of Raasay to slay him. He promised him as a reward all the land from Uig to Portree, a distance of fifteen miles by road. MacLeod of Raasay, disguised as a beggar, obtained admittance to the monastery, slew the abbot, cut off his head, and set out for MacDonald's castle to claim his reward. But now MacDonald regretted his promise and his men gave battle to MacLeod of Raasay and his followers on a knoll above Lochan nan Ceann. The MacLeods were slain to a man and their heads as they were lopped off by strokes of the claymore rolled into the loch, which was afterwards named Loch of the Heads.

The loch has now been drained, but a psychic impression of that old fight may remain, and be visible to those who have 'the sight' when conditions are favourable.

A great tempest upon the Plain of Ler;
bold across its high borders
winter has arisen, fierce winter has slain us.

RUMAN'S SONG
From an old Celtic MS.

December is rarely a month of frost and snow; more often a succession of mild, moisture-laden winds from the south and south-west hold revel. I write on December 15, 1942, and in the Isle of Skye the grass is green and growing, and hydrangeas, which here survive the most severe winter outside, are still in flower in the wind-swept garden. The grass is green not only on the low ground; the corries of the hills are more verdant than they ever are in April, and often are in May. A true saying indeed is it that 'as the day lengthens the cold strengthens'. In the West Highlands the months of November and December, and sometimes January too, might be termed the months of the rainy season rather than winter. The days are short and the storm-laden wind rushes past everlastingly. No window is able to keep out that rain, driven on the gale at a velocity of sixty miles an hour and perhaps more. Pools of water creep out over the floors of the rooms on the weather side of the house or a miniature waterfall suddenly descends from the ceiling near my head as I sit at my desk; the house shakes and the wind roars in the chimneys so that Dara forsakes her usual comfortable bed on a rug before the peat fire and in discomfort and draught lies as far as possible from the fire and the wind-haunted chimney.

Talking (or rather writing) of Dara makes me remember that in the last chapter I had meant to write also of her predecessor, Dileas (the word is pronounced *Jeelus*, and is Gaelic for Faithful). Dileas was a collie from the Isle of Mull, black and white, lightly built and swift of foot. She was our constant, most devoted companion for many years, a remarkable dog in many ways. Dara is a philosopher, and her appetite never fails. Dileas had a more sad nature, and the sight of a suitcase being packed used to cause her grave disquiet, until she realised that she was to accompany us on the journey. She knew by name each member of the family, and when told to go to any particular one did so without hesitation. Like Dara she loved the water, was an accomplished swimmer, and liked retrieving a stick. Dara, when she has brought the stick to land, soon drops it and takes no further interest in it, but Dileas used to carry the stick for miles; on one occasion she carried a small fir branch through the Lairig Ghru pass all the way from Mar to Rothiemurchus. I remember that on one occasion she greatly impressed Ralph Armstrong, for many years head stalker to the Duke of Portland at Langwell. We were staying at Langwell, my wife and I, at the time, and were out on the hill with Ralph. When we were eating our lunch he was sitting a little way from us, out of our sight. He had in his game bag a couple of oranges which we wished to eat. We wrote our wants on a piece of paper, and told Dileas to go and find Ralph, which she did. He read the paper which had been put inside her collar and brought us what we had asked for. I find that most people think our two collies remarkable in their intelligence, but of this I am doubtful. The average dog owner does not develop the dog's intelligence; dogs, like human beings, have heights in their nature which they rarely reach, but which we can help them to attain. A dog can be a great friend and companion —almost one's greatest friend and companion in some respects.

At last our beloved Dileas fell sick of a mortal illness. Each morning she, like Dara, was accustomed to accompany me to the sea for a swim. That morning she came with me a short distance, very, very sorrowful, then turned back. She was more than sorrowful; she was in despair, for full well she knew that she was shortly going out on that long journey which would separate her from those she loved. She had sat in 'hides' with us as we watched the golden eagle; she had listened to the love song of the greenshank and had seen the ptarmigan rise from the high corries of the Cairngorms. She had accompanied us in the track of the hill blizzard and beneath the hot summer sun and had heard the thunder roll between Braeriach and Sgoran Dubh. Her life had been bound closely to our lives and now she knew she was going, to an unknown land, far from us both. Her look of sadness and despair remains with me after more than twelve years. That day I had to be from home, but my wife remained with Dileas. In the afternoon I knew there was sadness in my home, and knowing this I was ready for the news I received when I returned. That night we wrapped our beloved Dileas in her faded tartan rug, which had been her bed for many years, and when we had dug her grave we laid her to rest in it and built a cairn of stones over her body. I write 'over her body' advisedly, for I am sure that dogs, like human beings, are not extinguished by the great experience called Death, but go on to the world yonder which holds the spirit forms of trees and flowers, rivers, lakes and seas, birds and animals, and all those beings that we see in their material form on this earth. And so perhaps we shall some day find Dileas again.

During the years we have been together my wife and I have had three faithful dog companions. The first of the three—and I think the most

remarkable of the three—was Calum MacFadyen. He was a Dandy
Dinmont terrier, and came to us, as a very small puppy, at the beginning of our married life. He lived with us little more than two years
and endeared himself to us in an unusual degree.

He was exceptional, almost unique, I should think, among dogs in
having a sense of humour. If he saw that we were depressed or sad he
would deliberately set about performing for our benefit antics which
he knew would amuse. He had a much more buoyant and cheerful
nature than Dileas and had a superabundance of spirits. Like Dileas and
Dara he was passionately fond of the water and loved to retrieve a stick
thrown in for him. He had a contempt for the big waves, which sometimes broke over and engulfed him with no ill effects. A year before he
died he ate fish poisoned with strychnine: his life was saved only by
devoted nursing on the part of my wife, and I do not think his power
of resistance was the same after that. This happened at Kingstown in
Ireland where I was stationed at the time, and the following summer
during the severe influenza epidemic—it was in 1918, when that
deadly epidemic visited not only Europe but the whole world—he
developed pneumonia and died. His death was a profound sorrow to us
both. A day, or a couple of days, after he had gone I was on night duty
at the Naval Centre, and in the middle of the night, at the farther end
of the room and resting in space above the foot of my bed, I saw
Calum as we had always known him, but radiant and in shining glory.
That was nearly twenty-five years ago, yet I can still recall the spirit—
for I have no doubt it was the spirit—of our faithful companion come
to bid me farewell before he was borne on spirit wings far from the
material world where his short, happy life had ended. It is, I suppose rare
for any man, or any woman to have had during a quarter of a century
three dogs so greatly loved as Calum MacFadyen (sometimes called
Tine or Tinny Dewl) Dileas (sometimes called Dileas Bochd) and Dara
(sometimes called the Dragon Queen).

Although December in the main is a moist, mild month, short-lived
spells of frost and snow arrive with little warning. During the
early days of December, 1942, I happened to be in Aberdeenshire, on
upper Deeside, and the morning after I arrived awoke to a white
world. Less than an inch of snow covered the ground and the frost
lasted for only three days, yet on the third morning the river Dee at
Cambus O' May was frozen from bank to bank for a distance of perhaps
three hundred yards. During spells of frost quantities of floating ice,
called grue, float down the river, and if a coating of ice forms across a
still pool the floating grue brought up against it, being constantly rein-

forced, soon begins to spread up-stream, and in its turn is consolidated. Considerable stretches of the river are thus quickly frozen, even where the current is swift and no ice could form in the ordinary way. In the shallows where stones are near, or above the surface the drifting ice is pressed and consolidated, and rises, white and glistening, into the air in the form of miniature icebergs. As I stood on a bridge over quiet, clear water, where the river was not entirely frozen across, I saw two salmon, each perhaps twenty pounds in weight, lying beneath six feet of icy water on the stony river bed; a few yards from them was a smaller fish of about six pounds. When I passed that way again later in the day the fish were still in the same place. Although salmon are cold-blooded creatures they undoubtedly feel the cold, although they are not inconvenienced by it in the way warm-blooded animals are. It has, rather, the effect of making them torpid and lethargic. Anglers for salmon know that the lower the river temperature the larger is the fly that must be used, and the deeper it must be fished. Indeed the first thing an experienced gillie will do on a January, February or March morning before the size of fly is decided on is to take the river temperature, and from it make his decision.

December is the one month in the year when the salmon devotee is not permitted by law to throw his fly on any Scottish river, for the Tweed closes its waters at dusk on November 30, and the opening day of the Tay, that prince among early spring Highland rivers, is on January 15, although certain northern rivers are open a week before that. There is no better relaxation for war-weary men and women than angling, for the thoughts of the angler are wholly engrossed in his art, and the murmur of the stream, and the song of river birds like the dipper soothe the senses.

Writing of the dipper recalls to my mind the remarkable feat of this sprightly white-bellied bird of black plumage, of habitually walking beneath the water along the river bed. While submerged beneath two or three feet of water it is able to move with its bill small stones in order to feed upon the caddis-flies hidden below them; therefore, so long as the river remains open, the dipper is able to find food when frost and snow are telling heavily on land birds. In winter the river Ness is haunted by large numbers of dippers, or water ousels as they are usually called in Scotland. The Ness flows from that great fresh-water loch, Loch Ness, and, like the loch, never freezes. Hear what an old account, taken from Vol. I of MacFarlane's Geographical Collections, says of Loch Ness:

'This Lake never freezeth and if a lump of ice is cast into it, it soon after dissolveth. Its commonly thought on this account, it runs on sulphureous minerals, though it may be otherways as it is with our springs of water, which either through constant motion, pressure of the aire, or the heat retiring itself in time of cold does not allow them to freeze. This being still observed, that in time of frost or when high winds are or shortly to be, they are warme and in hott weather or calm, they are cold. Whether there may be betwixt deep lakes or springs running through the bowells of hills a subterraneous communication with the ocean . . . I will not take upon me to determine.'

The water ousels of the Ness thus know that their food supply will never be cut off from them by the frost, and may be seen fearlessly disporting themselves even where the river flows through the heart of the town.

That December morning on which I had watched the salmon in the frost-bound Dee, when they had seemed weighed down by torpor and lethargy, I thought how different must have been their behaviour when, fresh from their feeding grounds in the depths of the Atlantic, they had swiftly approached the coast of Scotland, travelling, it is believed, from the north west. By netting fish in the sea and returning them marked to the water again the Fishery Board for Scotland have brought interesting facts to light regarding the speed at which a salmon travels. Of seven salmon marked in the sea off Loch Inchard in North West Sutherland two were taken the same season in the nets at the mouth of the Aberdeenshire Dee, and five were taken farther south, off the coast of Montrose. A grilse marked off Loch Laxford was caught by rod and line on the river Tay at Murthly, 290 miles away, the same season. Another salmon marked on the coast of North West Sutherland was recaptured a little later in the same season off Whitby in Yorkshire, but a more remarkable record was that of a fish marked at the same place and caught again in a bag net off the Sognefjord in Norway, for this salmon had to travel across the ocean from Scotland to Norway and the distance from Cape Wrath in Scotland to Sognefjord in Norway is fully 400 miles, not counting the swim along the north west seaboard of Scotland from Loch Inchard to Cape Wrath.

Some of the fish which were recovered in other districts after having been marked reveal the speed at which a salmon travels. A fish marked off the East Sutherland coast and recaptured off the Forth seven days later averaged thirty-five miles a day for that journey. One of the salmon marked off the North West Sutherland coast and caught again in the Forth averaged a distance of thirty-three miles a day. It is possible indeed that both these fish had been cruising in the Firth of Forth some little time before they were caught, and that therefore the average distance travelled daily may have been even greater than I have set down. These journeys, however, are as nothing compared to the voyage of a salmon marked in Norway by Professor Dahl. That fish covered a distance of 690 miles at an average speed of sixty-two miles a day. Another remarkable Norwegian record is a salmon which averaged thirty miles per day over the great distance of 1560 miles.

It is, I think generally admitted that a salmon in the ordinary course of events returns to the river where it was hatched: the race of salmon which inhabit the various Highland rivers show slight differences, so that an expert can pick out in a fishmonger's shop a Tay salmon, a salmon of the Dee, a Ness fish, and so on. During the summer of 1942 I was fishing the Laxford in Sutherland, and on my return saw a number of salmon which had been netted in the Staffin River in Skye, and there was an unmistakable difference between the fish of these rivers which, by sea, are no more than seventy miles distant. The average size of the Laxford salmon has been considerably increased by stocking the river with ova from the Shin and Tay, and now fish of over forty pounds in weight are caught in it.

On the December morning when I watched the salmon in the river Dee I recalled one of the finest fishermen of the old school in the Highlands. He was Admiral Sir Arthur Farquhar, one of a celebrated naval family whose younger members still carry on with distinction their family calling. I recall Arthur Farquhar landing nine salmon out of one pool of upper Dee during a single afternoon. So far as I know, however, he did not practice the latest method of salmon fishing—the greased line method, the most skilled exponent of which was the late Arthur Wood of Cairnton. Arthur Farquhar was one of the most lovable men I have known, and one of those people who never grow old in spirit; on a winter morning at the age of eighty I have seen him wash his car before driving himself after breakfast to the course for a round of golf. He was a great bird lover and student all his long life and told me that wherever he went, and on whatever ocean he was sailing, he was never lonely, for his friends the birds were always there for him to watch and study. He said that on one occasion his knowledge of the habits of birds stood him in good stead. He was bringing his squadron into the Firth of Forth and a thick fog lay upon the sea so that it was not easy to steer a correct course. But by watching the gannets overtaking his ship and passing ahead, and by watching the course those birds were on, he was able to check his position, for he realised, from his knowledge of their habits, that the destination of the gannets must be the Bass Rock.

The Admiral was a great lover of the hills, and I thought how he would have enjoyed watching the sunrise on the summit of Lochnagar, the highest hill of the Balmoral deer forest, that morning. Sunrise, especially by our war Summer Time in winter, is indeed late in December, and it was not until almost ten o'clock that, happening to look westward up the Dee valley, I saw the high slope and summit of the hill flushed with deep rose. Earlier that morning those snowy slopes were cold and grey, but the sun when it reached them transformed them to a rich warm glow. That evening, a few minutes before sunset, the snowy country was bathed in a violet glow, rare and beautiful to see and resembling the light of the Arctic. Lochnagar is not the old name for this hilltop, but the loch which lies deep in its corrie is called Lochnagar, and the name has gradually been given to the hill also. Professor W. J. Watson, perhaps the greatest authority upon Celtic place-names, tells me that the name of the loch in its original form is Loch na Gàire, Loch of the Outcry, and that this name has been given it because of the moaning of the wind amongst the rocks.

The song thrush or mavis migrates from Upper Deeside in winter, but some of the blackbirds remain. I noticed a cock blackbird haunting the playground of Crathie school one afternoon when the ground was iron-hard; no doubt he had been feeding on the crumbs left by the scholars after their lunch (the more advanced students travel down the Dee valley to school at Ballater, crowding the morning bus and filling it with chatter and laughter).

The old forest of Scots pine which in bygone days covered the greater part of the Highlands is still seen on Upper Deeside. From the centuries-old outpost pines in Glen Luibeg and Glen Derry that forest extends eastwards through Mar to Balmoral and even east of that place to Glen Tana (the Thin Glen) and Finzean, where Farquharson of Finzean, chief of the clan, formerly lived.

The war, alas, is bringing disaster upon that old forest. Everywhere the woodman's axe is working havoc among trees which were vigorous at the time of Culloden and beneath which the remnants of the fleeing Jacobite army perhaps sheltered. From the Black Wood of Rannoch, far to the west, to Glen Feshie, Mar and Balmoral the splendid old pines are being felled. Had this been done in time of Peace a storm of criticism would have been aroused, but in wartime the power of the individual to criticise is lost. At all events let us hope that the pines, after being felled, will not be left to bleach and decay. This happened after the so-called Great War of 1914–18 in the forest of Glenmore at the foot of the Cairngorms. Two years and more after the close of that war the trees, as I myself saw, lay where they had been thrown to earth. They were, it seemed, felled too far from the sawmill to make it profitable to drag them there. Let us hope that this will be avoided in the present emergency.

It is curious that some parts of the old Caledonian Forest should show the phenomenon of Natural Regeneration and that others should not. Natural Regeneration in simple language means a crop of young trees, grown from seed scattered by their elders, springing up beneath their parents so that, in the course of time, they take their place and the forest lives on. In the Forest of Abernethy the young trees are numerous and healthy, yet in the Forest of Mar, across the Cairngorm range, scarcely a young seedling pine is to be seen. This is attributed, and I think rightly, to the activities of the red deer, which in hard weather eat the seedlings. I have often urged those responsible that areas here and there should be fenced in against the deer until such time as the young trees have made a good start, but nothing has been done and it is now perhaps too late. There are many unsightly woods of planted trees after these five years of war and felling, still standing in the Highlands. It is curious that these woods should have been left and the natural forest, a priceless possession to us, should, in places, have been almost wiped out. The chief sufferer from the denudation of this ancient forest must be the crested tit. The small crested titmouse has its firm home in the depths of the old pine forest; summer and winter it remains in the shelter of the pine canopy. It is a stay-at-home little bird, otherwise it must surely have crossed the passes of the Cairngorms from Strathspey to where, scarcely a dozen miles away, the outposts of the Mar pines would afford it shelter. But, so far as I know, the crested tit has never been seen in the old pine forest of Mar, or the equally old pine forest of Ballochbuie on the Balmoral ground.

Unexpected birds cross the Cairngorms on migration. Robins, I think, must have a flight line over this hill range. In one of my books I have mentioned finding a robin lying lifeless on deep snow at the Pools of Dee in spring. In the summer of 1941 a friend of mine showed me two mummified small birds she had found on the high Cairngorms. One of the birds was a robin, the other, strangely enough, a bullfinch, a bird associated with gardens and young plantations rather than the wind-swept summits of a high hill range. That bullfinch was light as a feather: it had evidently been lying on the hill for some time, yet the beauty of its small red breast was unimpaired. These fragile birds had no doubt been caught in mist and driven snow on their migration across the Cairngorms, and had been choked by the drift which, as I know by experience, might prove equally deadly to the human wanderer caught by it far from shelter.

I have mentioned the crested tit as likely to be one of the chief sufferers by the felling of the old pines, but other birds also will be left homeless. The siskin, the crossbill and, to name a great lordly bird, the capercaillie, will suffer. The siskin is so small, and so timid, or perhaps I should say elusive, that it is not well known. Last summer I was staying in a house at the edge of the forest and on the gravel outside that house I saw one day a flock of siskins feeding actively on what seemed to be the seeds of a few grass weeds. It was interesting and unusual to look out at these small birds from such close quarters; but all too soon that low, vulgar and thoroughly reprehensible bird the house sparrow appeared on the scene and like a giant swooped down angrily on the little flock, scattering its members in flight, nor did I see them again although I hoped they would return.

The crossbill has, I think, increased in the old forest during recent years. The Highland tradition, that its bill became crossed and twisted from its efforts to draw out the nails which bound Christ to the Cross, may have some counterpart in the folklore of other European nations. The rich red on the breast of the male crossbill is said to commemorate the stain of Christ's blood, which reddened the plumage while the bird was engaged on its work of pity. Ornithologists have now decided that there are two races of crossbills, the Continental crossbill and the Scottish crossbill, or rather British crossbill: the continental form visits us in the autumn on migration. A flock of crossbills feeding in the crown of a pine is an arresting sight: the birds, with their specially contrived bills, are adepts at extracting the seeds from the cones which they then allow carelessly to fall to the ground.

In the Caledonian forest the capercaillie has its home. The male caper is a grand bird, and when he is disturbed in the depths of the pine forest and flies fast and sure through the trees he looks almost as big as an eagle. The old race of Highland capercaillies became extinct early in the nineteenth century. In an Aberdeen paper of the year 1838 is the following note, describing the attempts then being made to introduce a new race of these birds from Sweden:

'The Earl of Fife is the fortunate possessor of a live male capercailzie and three females of this magnificent bird, and a couple are at present affectionately engaged in rearing a hopeful progeny of no less than seven young ones.'

Again the same paper notes, in the same year:

'We are happy to learn that the capercali which . . . Lord Breadalbane turned out into his forests in Scotland during the past and present summer have bred in those wilds. There were 44 altogether. This splendid collection was made in Sweden with vast trouble and at very great expense by Mr. Lloyd.'

In the *Kilmarnock Journal*, of the year 1842, is an interesting note that capercaillie's eggs sent from the Marquis of Breadalbane to the Duke of Hamilton at Brodick Castle in the Isle of Arran had been placed under 'moorgame' for hatching. There is a contemporary record that a pair of capercaillies were shot at Wick in the year 1838. These were evidently two of the imported birds, and the record is interesting since Wick is in treeless country, nor is there any likely capercaillie ground for many miles around. It looks as if that pair of birds were endeavouring to make their way back to their home country, guided by such homing instinct as they possessed. In early spring the cock caper works himself into a frenzy or ecstasy of love as he perches at dawn on the branches of some pine or spruce. I have not heard this love song, if song it can be termed, in the Scottish Highlands but have heard it in the Schwarzwald of Germany, a good many years ago now. The grand finale of the song I chiefly remember; it is impressed upon my mind as a violent and prolonged sneeze. During that final note, or series of notes, the cock capercaillie is blind and deaf because of his love ecstasy; the hunter or stalker takes advantage of this and each time the song is uttered runs a little nearer to his quarry, remaining motionless during the songless intervals and trusting to the half light to conceal his form from the singer. The hen caper is a quiet-plumaged bird, considerably smaller than the male, and not unlike a giant greyhen. Indeed a caper cock and a greyhen have been known to mate and produce a hybrid family.

The main haunts of the capercaillie are in the Central Highlands. One autumn morning I was being driven down the avenue of Glentruim House in the Badenoch district of the county of Inverness. Ahead of the car a large bird sedately and without haste walked across the avenue. It was very light on the back—slate grey and white—and for a moment I thought it was some exotic fowl, yet a nearer view told me that this was no stranger but a capercaillie hen, unusually light in colour. Capers are sometimes very tame and I heard of a capercaillie cock in Rothiemurchus forest which was of a pugilistic temperament and liked nothing better than to attack a lady from the rear, aiming vicious pecks at her legs, especially if they were encased in thin silk stockings.

In the last chapter I wrote a little about Buteo the buzzard, which is on the increase throughout the Highlands at the present day. In the Isle of Skye I see the buzzard almost daily. Only this afternoon, as the early December dusk was dimming the soft light of a mild December day, I saw a buzzard appear beneath me where I sat near a hilltop overlooking the Minch. A fresh south-east wind was blowing, and the buzzard, rising in spirals, was literally shot into the air by the uprising wind currents. He climbed in spirals as the eagle climbs, but was not so steady or lordly in his flight. I noticed that after spiralling for a time from right to left he checked his flight, fluttered a little, then began to spiral from left to right; perhaps he was a little giddy. When he had reached a considerable height and had passed above the up-draught caused by the hill he set a course for a neighbouring cliff, planing there without effort or wing movement. I have often thought how easy the greater birds of prey find it to progress, merely by utilising the up-rising wind currents of the hill country to which they belong.

Seeing the buzzard going to roost at five o'clock in the afternoon made me realise what a short day's food-hunting a bird has in December. It is not really light (I refer to the Highlands of Scotland) until ten o'clock in the morning by Summer Time and little hunting by a bird of prey can be done after four in the afternoon. The period during which no food can be found is therefore not far short of 18 hours. But the larger Raptores are perhaps more fortunate than smaller birds, for in winter many a braxy sheep succumbs on the hillside, and the buzzards may feast with impunity upon the carcases, unless warned off by a patrolling raven, which is almost always the buzzard's master.

A friend who returned from a day's shooting only a few hours before these notes were written told me that he surprised a buzzard in the act of killing a red grouse for its supper. On his approach the buzzard flew away, leaving the grouse, which was still warm, and was added to my friend's 'bag'. Indeed it was the only grouse he saw that day. In fairness to the buzzard it must be stated that it does not habitually feed on grouse; even if it were so minded it is not a sufficiently active bird to make a practice of grouse killing: it preys mainly upon rabbits, rats and mice and, as I have mentioned, enjoys carrion. Bird protectionists weaken their case by ignoring, or glossing over facts. It cannot truthfully be said that *any* bird of prey will *never* touch game. But it can be said that certain of the clan—for example the peregrine falcon—*habitually* prey on game, while others, such as the buzzard and the kestrel, rarely do so.

On my homeward walk I passed a collection of small stunted willow bushes, growing on the east face of the hill where they had protection from the prevalent Atlantic storms from west and south west. A little flock of twites rose from these bushes and flew over my head. The twite is sometimes called the mountain linnet. Like some other birds— for instance the dunlin—it has two distinct habitats in Scotland. In the Central Highlands it frequents the high hills, where I have seen the nest and blue, delicately spotted eggs more than 3000 feet above the sea. But in the Western Highlands, and in the Inner and Outer Hebrides, the twite is a bird of the lesser hills and even of the level country of the sea coast. In the Outer Hebridean island of South Uist trees are few and far between, but in the garden of Grogary Lodge escallonia bushes afford some slight shelter from the ocean storms. In these bushes, and in the stone wall which surrounds the garden, twites make their nests, and the cheery little song of the male twite as he sails down to his perch rather like a tree pipit mingles with the sighing of the wind (which here is seldom at rest) in the bushes. How fragile a being is the twite compared with the grey geese which so often pass in measured flight over that wind-swept house, or with the sharp-winged golden plover which are seen for a moment and are gone, or with the complaining tribe of the curlew, or the whimbrel, passing northward in May on migration to Iceland.

Cold the winter night is, the wind is risen, the high couraged, un-quelled stag is on foot: bitter cold to-night the whole mountain is, yet from all that the ungovernable stag is belling.

SILVA GADELICA

At the threshold of the new year, after prolonged mild weather from the south west, came a morning of keen frost. A steamy vapour rose from the limpid Dee as it hurried on its seaward course; chaffinches and the clan of the titmice flitted among the pines. As I climbed above the Dee at Crathie, I came to milder air, and at the edge of the pine forest the quiet pools beneath the trees were scarcely touched by the frost which held sway in the valley below, although thin fingers of black ice were slowly feeling their way across their clear water. The road rose still higher, and now a snow bunting took flight on white wings ahead of me and moved low, almost furtively, along the road, keeping below the tops of the heather that grew beside it. A herd of hinds, with two or three stags amongst them, were climbing the hill to the east of where I stood; as they crossed the pass I could see that the stags were distressed by the ascent (although it was not steep) and panted like dogs after a chase: the hinds were apparently in better training and their mouths were scarcely open.

I now stood in sight of the Cairngorm range. Cairntoul, Braeriach and Beinn a' Bhuird were clear, but at first mist hid Ben MacDhui, highest of them all. It was a cloud born of the glens rather than of the high tops, and for a brief space that bare, rounded summit, stern and wild, was seen above the rose-coloured mist, lighted by the winter sun. Then the cloud flowed in upon it, and it was gone. There was little snow on the high hills, although drifts lay in some of the corries: Lochnagar had scarcely a speck of snow upon it.

I hoped that I should find the golden eagle at his hunting and, sure enough, it was not long before I saw him, moving with deliberation about a hundred feet above the hill across which the herd of deer had recently passed. Using the uprising current from the hill, the eagle sailed without effort aslant the wind. I watched him, at first with my unaided eyes, then through a stalking glass, until he was a dark speck in the distance. I knew that a deerstalker was out after hinds in that direction, and when at last I saw the eagle check his flight and begin to sail in spirals, I imagined that he had sighted the stalking party, and was hopeful of a feed from the gralloch of a hind. On my homeward walk I again saw my snowbunting friend by the road, and at the edge of the pine wood a greyhen rose from the heather and flew off with graceful, unhurried flight above the trees that now swayed in the hill wind which had arisen and was bringing dark clouds to the Cairngorms and to the high corries of Ben A'an across the river.

That morning came near the end of the fine weather; the New Year was no more than a day old when the wind veered to the north and all the Highlands, from the Dee westward to Skye and the Outer Isles, lay beneath a coat of snow. It was early afternoon when the snow ceased, the sky cleared, and across the Minch, inky blue beneath the heavens, the hills of Harris rose white-clad and beautiful against the dark clouds that lay beyond them. On the first day of that New Year (1943) some of the Skye crofters had not begun to lift their potatoes: the autumn and early winter had been, it is true, unusually wet, yet it seemed to me that the crop with diligence might have been lifted ere then.

After a short period of north wind a frosty spell began. The Minch at length was calm, and the crofters living beside the sea lost no time in setting their drift nets for herring. When I reached the shore I found that one boat had landed four crans of herrings; the fish lay in a silvery heap at the bottom of the boat, among them one or two small dog-fish and a small coal fish. We rowed out into the Minch, and at the back of the high rocky isle known as Eilean Tuilm lifted a trammel net set the previous day. When we lifted it we found in its meshes fourteen pollack or lythe, several dogfish, and a small lobster. Another victim was an unfortunate shag, which on one of its diving expeditions had become firmly entangled in the net. When we returned to the landing place we found that the neighbouring crofters had heard of the herring catch and had appeared on the scene. They were buying the herrings for twenty shillings the basket (a basket is a quarter of a cran) and were very glad to get them, as owing to the tempestuous early winter fish had been unobtainable. The dogfish were thrown back into the sea for, even under war conditions, this fish is not eaten in the west Highlands, although when they are caught in sufficient numbers they are sent to the markets of the mainland. Dogfish are tenacious of life: they were too weak to swim away, but their pig-like eyes glared balefully at their captors: one of them feebly swam under a stone and there kept its station despite the suck of the small waves; with returning strength it doubtless soon swam away into deep water. The small lobster, also weak, walked delicately backwards but remained in the shallows: a frosty air is soon fatal to the lobster tribe if they are out of the water.

Lobsters were very scarce around the Hebridean Isles that winter.

Herring Gulls soaring against the wind over the Island of Lambay.

The old wooden handplough, known as the Cas Chrom, is still in use in the Western Highlands and Islands.

It may be that the oil which polluted the waters of all the seven seas was the reason for their scarcity. On one occasion when the local crew of fishermen lifted their creels their catch, from fifty lobster pots, was only two lobsters! Lobsters, because of the scarcity of other fish, were then, just before the price was controlled, fetching unheard of prices in the market: 8/6 per pound was the price offered, which meant that a good-sized lobster was worth at least £1. Lobsters of five pounds are not uncommon: in the summer of 1942 I heard of a giant of eleven pounds being taken off the coast of the Isle of Mull. Another of the same weight was caught some years ago in a trammel net on the north-west coast of Skye. But even those two monsters were small as compared to the giant caught off the west of the Isle of Mull by A. MacDougall in 1921. That lobster weighed fifteen pounds and was sold for £5. These great lobsters are too large to enter the trap through the hole: they are usually found clinging to the outside of the lobster creel, and so reluctant are they to relinquish their claim to the tasty bait within that they permit themselves to be drawn to the surface and caught by hand.

In January most creeping things are in the depths of hibernation. When I was taking in peats from the peat stack I came upon a pair of earwigs guarding their eggs, laid below one of the damp peats at the outside of the stack. It was a mild day and one of the earwigs made off: the other remained beside the eggs as though on guard. It kept quite motionless, its antennae held over the yellow eggs protectingly, and there I left it.

The oil on the sea which, as I have said, may account for the scarcity of lobsters, is proving deadly to seabirds. That winter the little auk was the chief sufferer. I found one of these attractive little birds preening its oiled plumage at the edge of the tide. It took no notice of me until I picked it up. As I carried it along the shore I noticed that when a larger wave than usual broke in thunder the little auk in my hand went through the movements of 'oaring' with its wings. I do not think it trusted me to avoid the wave, and was preparing itself for the water should we both be caught.

The bird was cleaned and dried but lived for less than a week. One morning when I visited it its cold body lay in its box: its spirit during the hours of darkness had as I knew escaped, free as air, to fly to, and alight on, a spirit sea. It is true that cures are sometimes effected with these oiled sea birds, but they are very, very few in number, and I am inclined to think that it is better to leave the oiled victims beside the friendly sea where death will quietly overtake them while they are still free, rather than carry them to unknown and mistrusted surroundings where it is not easy for them to understand the irksome administrations of those who are endeavouring to restore them to health.

On the coast, these winter days, a large and handsome black and white bird, goose-like in appearance and in size, may sometimes be seen. Its haunts are low shores where the tide sweeps in at the flood through the short-cropped salt-resisting vegetations to form muddy pools or a soft ooze. Here the shelduck, for this is the bird of which I write, has its home, summer and winter. Both female and male of the species sport a bright red berry or knob at the base of the upper mandible; the sexes indeed are almost indistinguishable, which is unusual in the duck tribe. But the female shelduck has not, like the mallard, the tufted duck, teal and most other wildfowl, to rely for safety on her protective coloration when she is brooding her eggs. She makes her home deep down at the end of a burrow on the sand dunes where she is safe from the unwelcome visits of gulls and crows, and other egg-stealing birds, and therefore her plumage of black, white and rich brown is no dis-service to her. Shelducks lay large clutches of eggs and are model parents. Remarkably large broods are sometimes recorded, but a friend recently told me of what must be almost a record number. He said that outside his house as he wrote he could see a pair of shelducks with no fewer than forty-three young ones! Shelducks and eiders have a habit of annexing, whether inadvertently or deliberately I cannot say, the brood of a neighbour, but it would seem as though this particular pair of birds were rearing at least three broods.

A friend of mine recently showed me a pair of grouse with white primary wing feathers, which he had shot on the island of Hoy, one of the Orkney group. I was speaking to Mr. George Arthur of Kirkwall on the subject. He is an experienced ornithologist, and told me that a number of years ago several broods of ptarmigan had been reared under grouse on the heathery slopes of Hoy. He said that the birds seemed to acclimatise themselves, although the highest part of Hoy is little more than 1000 feet above the sea, and therefore much lower than their natural haunts: for some years the birds were seen on the isle, but they were gradually killed off. It would be interesting to know whether that pair of white-winged grouse were relics of the race. In December 1930 a white grouse was seen on the moor at Delnadamph, Strathdon. It disappeared at the end of March 1931, but appeared again in October: no one knew where it had been during the intervening months. On February 17, 1943, Alexander MacHardy, gamekeeper at Delnadamph, Strathdon, wrote me that a pack of grouse was seen and in it a white grouse: he wondered if it were the same bird. The Cairngorms are the headquarters of British ptarmigan, and here the lowest-nesting ptarmigan and the highest-nesting grouse are often found on the same ground, and although it might be thought that the two races, closely allied as they are, would at times interbreed. I have never seen a hybrid. Ptarmigan have a world-wide distribution, from Spitsbergen to the Himalayas, but the red grouse in its true wild state is found nowhere but in Britain. It is indeed the only bird which we can claim as our very own. There seems to be no doubt that the red grouse gradually sprang from ptarmigan or willow grouse stock. As the ice age receded the snow rarely lay for long on the lower moors, and it was therefore no longer necessary for these birds of the lower hills to assume a winter plumage of white. Thus, in the course of long ages, the red grouse as a species was born. It is, for the Highlands, a most valuable bird and brings, or brought, more money into that district than the red deer.

But the old days, and the old race of Highlanders, are fast passing. The Highland deerstalker was a grand type. He had a strong personality, a keen sense of humour, was of a fine integrity and most loyal in friendship. English was with him an acquired language and he spoke it sometimes quaintly and often forcibly. I remember that after a cold sunless season a stalker was telling me of the weather that had been experienced in his glen. He said, 'At times it would appear as though the sun were to gain the *masterpiece*, but then the wind would get *up*, the mist would come *down*, and the atmosphere would become most *ungenial*.'

Two old worthies of this kind one Saturday evening boarded a local train and entered my compartment. They had both had a good dram, and before long a discussion started as to the wing-spread of the golden eagle. I ventured to agree with the opinion of one as against the other. He in the minority looked at me rather doubtfully, and although he plainly thought I did not know what I was talking about he was too polite to say so. But his friend, who I had seen eyeing the label on my luggage, said to him quietly, 'Do ye know who yon is?' 'No, indeed' came the answer. 'Well', said the first in triumph, 'yon is Setton Gordon!' This remark was rather a score, for his convivial companion, remarking 'A'm din' (I'm done), ceased to argue more on the subject.

A grand man was Sandy MacDonald (he who locally went by the name of The Brogach, meaning The Lad), who for many years was stalker on the Derry beat of Mar Forest. When we lived at Aviemore Sandy walked through the Lairig Ghru to visit us. He had never seen the sea, and took the train to Inverness to look at it, but I remember that he was disappointed with his visit, for the ocean as seen from Inverness is not inspiring. I recall crossing the Lairig one September day with my friend, Major L. F. Hay of the Forty-Second Highlanders. Major Hay was six feet eleven in height, and easily the tallest man in the British Army. Sandy and the Prince of Wales (now Duke of Windsor) had been stalking and as we approached we saw them standing outside Sandy's cottage at Luibeg. The Prince came out to meet us (we both knew him well) and Sandy told me afterwards that they had been 'spying' us through their stalking glasses when we were still a good distance away, and that the Prince had told him that Major Hay and he had been through the early part of the 1914–1918 war in France together, and that it was strange that Major Hay, being the tallest man in the army, should have been wounded in the foot. That day they had been stalking on the high ground of Ben MacDhui, and their stalk was spoiled by a tourist who gave the deer his wind. The Prince said to Sandy, 'Shall I fire a shot a few hundred yards from him, Sandy, just to let him know there are stalkers on the hill?' 'Na, na, Your Royal Highness' replied Sandy 'it would maybe get into the *Daily* ——', mentioning a newspaper of socialistic leanings. All the stalkers told me that the Prince was a first-rate shot with a rifle, and better than his father King George V, whose marksmanship with a shot gun, as opposed to a rifle, was particularly good.

Shortly after the end of the 1914–1918 war, Sandy MacDonald found what he supposed to have been a bomb on the hillside behind his cottage. He took the object home, and one day that summer when the Prince of Wales was out stalking, he showed him the 'bomb'. The Prince sent it to the Air Ministry, where it was recognised as a flare and was later found to have been dropped by Zeppelin L 20 when over Mar Forest by night at the beginning of May, 1916. Sandy's son, Donald, at the early age of thirty years, became head stalker of Mar Forest; another son, Alick, is also stalker on that forest.

When I first knew the Derry there were two fine old stalkers there. One of them, Donald Fraser, lived in Derry Lodge, the other, John Macintosh, had his home in Luibeg Cottage. After John Macintosh came Sandy MacDonald, and after him Alick Grant, a piper and, in his younger days, a heavyweight athlete. Alick Grant's wife came of good Highland stock. Her father, John Stewart, a noted deerstalker of Atholl, accompanied Queen Victoria on her journey through Glen Tilt. Her eldest brother Peter was for many years head stalker to the late Duke of Atholl, and her eldest sister was the wife of a well-known Highland deerstalker of the old school, Donald Crerar, Ardverikie.

When I first stayed at Loch Builg Lodge, a remote stalking lodge in Invercauld Forest, and now a ruin, an eccentric old stalker, MacPherson by name, lived there alone, his only companion being a wee Cairn terrier named Toddles. Toddles was his inseparable companion but, as is the way with terriers, was not always obedient. I remember Mac-Pherson shouting at him 'Come *back*, Toddles'. This was followed by a few forcible remarks, usually ending with 'Got *tamn* you, Toddles!' But Toddles knew that the curse was kindly meant and did not, metaphorically speaking, turn a hair.

In Taylor's *Braemar Highlands*, published in 1869 (a book that is now difficult to buy) the local tradition for the name Invercauld is given, and as it is one which I have not heard elsewhere I mention it here. Invercauld, according to the tradition, is in its original Gaelic Inver Challa, River-mouth of the Defeat or Calamity. Here, it is said, the Laird of Rothiemurchus (who laid claim to the estate) and his men met in battle Finlaidh Mór, first of the Invercauld Farquharsons. A severe conflict ensued, the Rothiemurchus men were defeated, and their laird, Seumas na Gruag (James of the Flowing Hair) was killed at a place called the Craggins. The burn where the fight was fought was afterwards known as Allt a' Challa, and the burn-mouth Inverchalla.

The deerstalkers on the royal forest of Balmoral were all fine men. There was a rather curious custom that, when on the hill, the royal rank of the 'gentlemen' was temporarily forgotten, and they were addressed with a familiarity that would never have been thought of elsewhere. This familiarity was sometimes a shock to the ambassadors of foreign nations who were present. I recall on one occasion an ambassador of Spain hearing one of the stalkers say to the late King George V: 'You will bide here (showing him a place of concealment for the deer drive) but there's the Laddie (the Prince of Wales); I dinna know what we will dae wi' HIM.' It must of course have been on the initiative of the Royal Family that this lack of ceremony was the custom 'on the hill', for the Balmoral stalkers were courtly mannered men with a fine Highland dignity and bearing.

Charles Macintosh, second stalker on the Balmoral Forest, I knew well, and often stayed with him. It was he who, by supporting my weight on a ladder which he raised and held against his chest, enabled me to take my first photograph of a golden eagle's eyrie when I was a boy. His wife, I remember, was the baker of some of the finest scones I have tasted. Charles was an expert salmon fisherman. When the Court was not in residence at Balmoral the salmon caught were sent by passenger train to London, or to Windsor. In May and June, when the weather was warm and clear and the river was low, Charles Macintosh did his fishing after sunset and before sunrise, so that he had to be content with three or four hours' sleep, and sometimes even less, of a night. Many a fine salmon have I seen him take from the river in the early hours of the morning, when other folks were in bed and sound asleep. He was a great animal lover, and in his time had some beautiful collies and deer-hounds. I remember being on the hill with him and a particularly lovely collie bitch which he then had. We were sheltering behind a knoll—there was a strong wind blowing at the time—when we were surprised to see a dog fox coming towards us up-wind, sniffing the air and moving fast. The fox had almost reached us when he got our wind and reluct-antly turned away. Charles said that he had known the same thing happen before, and had no doubt that the dog fox had got the bitch's scent, and had been unable to distinguish it from the scent of a vixen in heat.

The morrell mushroom, chocolate-coloured and crinkled, grows plentifully in spring in the Ballochbuie Forest of Balmoral, and it was Charles Macintosh who first taught me that this was edible. He told me that the Duke of Edinburgh had once mentioned to him that this mushroom fetched a high price when sold in Berlin.

Since that day I have told many people about the morrell, and they have enjoyed eating it fried, when it has a kidney-like flavour. The morrell is one of the very few spring mushrooms which we have in the Highlands, and I do not remember having seen it anywhere except in the old pine forests. Its rich chocolate colour and wrinkled appearance make it easy to see above the carpet of pine needles where it is usually found.

The deerstalkers I have written of belonged to a past generation, but there are still men of the old tradition in the Highlands. George Ross, Gualann, Robert MacAulay and John Scobie, Lochmore, Finlay Macintosh, Ardverikie—these and others like them are carrying on the old standard of intelligent thinking, integrity and courtliness. But changed days are coming to the Highland deer forests and in some of them new men from the lowlands are being brought in to replace the old stock. I wonder what will be the fate of the deer forests during the next twenty-five years. It is true that a number of them came into being at the expense of the old population of the glens and straths. But that reprehensible policy of eviction was decided on a century and more ago and I am quite sure that under modern conditions the descendants of those who were evicted would not be willing to return and live where their forebears lived. If the forests went, the old families of deer stalkers would go with them—men who live very close to nature, who know each hill, each corrie, each burn; who understand the ways of the eagle and the ptarmigan, the fox, wild cat and marten; who know the lies of the salmon in the river pools and the haunts of the silvery sea-trout fresh from the tide. If these men go, the Highlands will have lost much of their charm—and yet I cannot see how the old landowning class in the Highlands will be able to retain their lands when the maelstrom of war is past.

Salmon fishing, on the other hand, will, I think, continue to be popular, for most people now sell their salmon and thus defray a considerable proportion of their expenses. January sees the opening of the salmon fishing. The Tay (with its tributary the Tummel) one of the best rivers of the Highlands, opens its waters on January 15. To fish for salmon in January one needs a considerable amount of stamina. A foot of snow may lie on the banks of the river, the wind may be bitter and frost-laden, and to ply the rod all day on an exposed river may on occasion be a feat of endurance. I think that even more endurance is required to sit in a boat all day—for this is how most of the salmon fishing on the lower Tay, where the river is broad and swift, is done. Boat fishing is called harling. The angler sits in a flat-bottomed boat and is rowed by two strong fishermen diagonally across the pool, from bank to bank, until the whole pool—and some of the Tay pools are of considerable extent—has been covered. The angler is usually in charge of three rods, a spinning rod on either side of the boat and a fly rod in the centre. One of the rods he holds, the other two 'fish' themselves, and on the line of each a small stone is placed, to 'strike' the salmon the moment it is hooked. Immediately a fish is hooked, the fisherman seizes the rod and the boatmen hurriedly reel in the lines of the other two rods. The boat is then rowed to the shore, where the angler plays the fish.

In January the rivers always hold numbers of kelts—spawned or 'spent' fish which have not returned to the sea. Sometimes they are a great nuisance, for they are greedier than clean-run salmon, and the fisherman may be playing and landing them the whole day long. It is not permissible to kill or even to gaff kelts; they must be tired out, then 'tailed' and returned to their natural element.

I once took a friend to fish the Tay on the opening day. He was a keen trout fisherman, but did not know much about salmon. We had an adventurous drive by car and after skidding and turning completely round on wet ice completed our journey in low gear and arrived two hours late at the river. Kelts that day were unusually plentiful. They were heavy fish and some of them were well-mended. They played well, and as each in turn had to be returned to the river my friend's disappointment grew. After playing one particularly well-mended kelt, which shone silvery as a fresh-run fish, he turned to me and said, 'That one was *very* nearly all right, wasn't it!' That remark impressed me, because I realised that he thought a salmon could gradually change back from a kelt to a clean fish in the river, and did not know that a prolonged stay in the sea was necessary to effect this change. As a matter of fact very few—less than two per cent—of the salmon of a river return to it after spawning. There is in the river after the spawning season a heavy mortality among male salmon but it seems remarkable that so few come back a second time. I have sometimes wondered whether the fish which return to the ocean after spawning may not remain there for the rest of their lives, feeding in plenty in mid-Atlantic, where are the ocean haunts of the species.

On the same Tay beat on a January day some years later I had a 32 lb. salmon, and my friend who was with me a beautiful 18-pounder. We played and landed in addition ten kelts and a large unspawned autumn hen fish during that short winter day.

When the angler is fortunate enough to hook a fresh-run salmon, he finds that it behaves differently to the kelts he has played hitherto. The kelts play and splash at the edge of the heavy water: the clean fish swims strongly and boldly out to the very middle of the river time after time and fights for his life in the strongest current; it takes longer to tire him than it takes to tire the heaviest kelt. A January clean-run salmon when he is landed lies on the bank like a bar of burnished silver; he more than repays hours of cold and discomfort beside the river and (in pre-war days) his capture was celebrated by a good dram of neat *uisge beatha*, shared between the angler and his gillie.

In January, when the herring fishing is successful, a considerable fleet lands its catches at Kyle of Lochalsh and Mallaig. Hundreds of herring gulls then make their winter quarters at these West Highland ports. If the observer watches carefully the wheeling flights of gulls as they circle time after time above the quay and the boats that are tied up to it he may see a bird of a similar size to the herring gulls, but with a different plumage. The feathers of this gull are creamy buff, and this plumage is much more attractive than the brown plumage of the immature herring gulls which so greatly outnumber it. This large cream-coloured bird is an immature Iceland gull. It is a wanderer from the north west and is usually seen singly amid great flocks of herring gulls in winter. Whoever named this bird the Iceland gull—and the name is an old one—was evidently unfamiliar with its habits, for the only known nesting country of the species is not Iceland but Greenland: it should therefore be the Greenland gull, but I suppose its present name has been attached to it too long for it to be changed now.[1]

The only other gull with which the Iceland gull might be confused is the glaucous gull, for the immature glaucous gull is also cream-coloured. But this is a very large bird, fully as big as our greater black backed gull, whose Arctic cousin indeed it is. The mature Iceland gull, and glaucous gull (they do not reach maturity until the fifth season) have pure white primaries. The fact that their wing-tips are white makes these birds look even larger than they are, for it must be remembered that the wing tips of the British herring gull, which might otherwise be confused with the mature Iceland gull, are black, with white 'mirrors'.

Glaucous gulls ascend the rivers of the Highlands in January and February to feed on the salmon which have died after spawning. In Spitsbergen the species nests sometimes on the low shingly shores of islands: one nest that I saw was built entirely of seaweed, and must have been at least two feet high.

In the West Highlands the flower traditionally associated with the month of January is the snowdrop. Below the deciduous trees which surround many of the old houses of the west the snowdrop spreads a great carpet white as snow. In the Isle of Skye the snowdrops of Tallisker and Kingsburgh are particularly fine. For some obscure reason the flowering of the snowdrops in 1943 in Skye was unusually late, although there was no snow all winter and only one week of frost. They were at least three weeks later than in 1941, when I saw an opened flower actually before New Year's Day. In 1943 I visited Kingsburgh on January 22, and few of the many thousands of flowers around the old house had then opened. I was told by the present owner that there is a strong tradition that the great array of flowers which each year beautify the grass around the house had their origin from a few bulbs brought home from the Crimea by an officer of a Highland regiment after the Crimean War. It may be remembered that Flora MacDonald, preserver of Prince Charles Edward, married MacDonald of Kingsburgh, and that Johnson and Boswell paid a visit to them there. It is possible that the MacDonalds were still at Kingsburgh at the time of the Crimean War and that it was one of this family who brought back the snowdrops from the Crimea. For forty-one years a single snowdrop flowered in the garden of St. Andrew's Manse at Tongue in Sutherland. It is mentioned in Bentham and Hooker's *British Flora* that the snowdrop flowers on the

[1] In late April 1944 an Iceland gull for some time made its home on the bay of Portree, Isle of Skye. It was almost fearless and I had an excellent close-up view of it.

Continent from the Caucasus to Holland, but that it is not, like the daffodil, a true native of Britain, although it is widely acclimatised there.

It is fortunate that garden pests such as mice leave the snowdrop alone. That winter, and the preceding one, we had a plague of mice. They stripped a winter cyclamen of its leaves and flower buds, ate down a clump of seedling primulas so that nothing remained of them, bit off at ground level each one of a group of carnation cuttings; and dug down to the bulbs of the tulips, to eat them also, although they did not apparently like daffodil buds.

On the Feast Day of beautiful Bride
The Flocks are counted on the moor;
The raven goes to prepare his nest.

OLD CELTIC SAYING

Féill Bhride, Saint Bride's Day, falls on the first day of February, old style—that is, on February 13 by our modern calendar. On that day the serpent, 'daughter of Ivor', is said to emerge for the first time from her hole in the heather or among the rocks. 'Bride with her white wand', writes Alexander Carmichael in *Carmina Gadelica*, 'is said to breathe life into the mouth of dead winter and bring him to open his eyes to the tears and the smiles, the sighs and the laughter of Spring.' On the Day of Saint Bride the dandelion, 'the little notched flower of Bride,' opens its first golden flower. One morning in early February I have gone out after a night of cold. The cold remained, yet in the air was that unmistakable scent—the birth of Spring.

At a time when universal war ravages the earth let us not forget the beauty of nature, the beauty of old traditions, the grandeur which dwells deep in the spirit of man.

As I write this chapter I have news of the most gallant rescue of a sheep dog on the great cliff of Tallisker, on the west of the Isle of Skye. Donald Cameron was with his two sheep dogs about three miles south of Tallisker. At the edge of the high sea cliff a large fox sprang from the heather ahead of him. His dogs gave instant chase, and all three disappeared over the cliff. Looking over the edge of the precipice the shepherd could see nothing: from a distant rock he could see the fox lying lifeless at the cliff foot, and his favourite dog, still alive, lying on a ledge about half way down the rock, which at this place is a full five hundred feet high. The rescue of the dog appeared hopeless, but repeated attempts were made by Mr. W. Wood, Customs Officer, Portree, and a lad of under eighteen, by name John MacDonald, from Tallisker.

The district is one of the most remote and storm-swept in Skye. The first attempt at rescue was abandoned because the rope was not sufficiently long; at the second attempt the gale was so violent that it was impossible to stand at the top of the cliff. It was at the third attempt that the epic rescue was successful. It was a day of bitter cold and the waves were leaping on the rocks five hundred feet below as the two rescuers, taking with them ropes and a pickaxe, worked their way down the cliff until they reached a narrow ledge about eighteen inches wide. They traversed this ledge for a considerable distance, hoping that it would lead them to a point above where the dog was lying. But the ledge petered out, and still they were not above the dog. They climbed back then to the top of the cliff and again descended with a piton and more rope. With the pickaxe, working under conditions of great danger, the rotten rock falling all about them, and upon them, they extended the ledge for a distance of some twelve feet. At last they were above the dog. Mr. Wood, an experienced rock climber, drove the piton into the rock and descended on a rope (John MacDonald steadying him with a second rope) to the ledge between thirty and forty feet beneath them where the dog was lying. Mr. Wood tied two ropes to the dog, which had now been eight days on the ledge and was very weak, and climbed back to the ledge. The two men after a rest then hauled the dog up to them and now began the perilous traverse of the ledge and the climb to the cliff top with the added burden of the dog. But at last safe ground was reached, and that evening, long after dark, the dog's master was overjoyed to see his faithful friend and companion with great excitement enter the door of his house.

This is one of the most daring rescues which I can imagine, for I know the Tallisker cliffs, and even in summer the feat would have been an outstanding one. In winter, when the rock is still more rotten because of frequent frosts, and the hands of the climbers must have been almost numb with the cold, the deed is the more admirable, and I am glad that the two climbers have been honoured by the Scottish Society for the Prevention of Cruelty to Animals.

It is a characteristic of the Highland shepherd that he is attached to his dogs. They are an important part of his life. Each day, in all weathers, they are out with him on hill and moor; he is dependent upon them for much of his work among the sheep. It was remarkable that Donald Cameron's dog succeeded in keeping a footing as it fell on that ledge half way down the cliff: his other dog, a young animal, went right over to the bottom and was not seen again. It is curious, too, that so intelligent an animal as a fox should have made that leap to its death: perhaps it was asleep when disturbed, and in the sudden excitement of seeing two dogs close upon it lost its head and its sense of direction.

Fox and golden eagle often frequent the same ground. The golden eagle is nominally protected in most parts of the Highlands, but this protection in fact is often withheld. A friend of mine, who owns a deer forest and protects his eagles, told me an amusing tale. He was travelling south from the Highlands, and in the dining car that evening sat opposite a stranger who in course of time entered into conversation with him and told him that he was pestered by—naming my friend's name—a certain gentleman's golden eagles, which came over to his moors and alarmed his grouse. Then he confided to the stranger that he had got even with this man, for he had caused pole traps to be set on his ground, and had succeeded in capturing in them more than one golden eagle. Thus on his own showing he had twice broken the law of the land. Pole traps, because of the deadly pain they inflict upon the creatures they catch, are illegal, and the golden eagle is also protected by law. My friend heard the unsavoury story out to the end, but did not divulge his identity. He went to the chief constable of the county, and told him the story. He was asked whether a witness had been present at the conversation: when the representative of the law learnt that the two had been alone he said he was afraid that nothing could be done in the matter. This goes to show that in the matter of bird protection the letter of the law is of little use and I believe that the deadly and illegal pole trap is actually becoming each year more numerous in the Highlands. Yet despite the traps set for it, and the egg collectors which each year rob many eyries known to me, the eagle is holding its own in the West Highlands although in the Central Highlands it is becoming scarcer. Where it is permitted to live out its wild, free life the eagle reaches a great age; my own belief is that a centenarian golden eagle is no uncommon thing.

Although the eagle is holding its own, the graceful hen harrier is now almost extinct on the mainland of Scotland as a nesting species, although each year migrants from the north are seen. The wings of the harrier are long, pointed and graceful; the tail also is long. The female is brown, with a pure white patch (prominent in flight) on the rump: the male is of a very lovely pearl grey. A friend has written to tell me of a battle he watched between a male harrier and a peregrine falcon. He was sheltering on a February day beneath a plantation of Scots pines near the shore of the Moray Firth when he heard angry yelps and barks overhead. A peregrine was mobbing a large grey bird which my friend thought at first was a herring gull. But his field glasses at once showed him that this was no gull but a glorious male hen-harrier in full plumage. Round and round went the two birds, the falcon, immensely superior in flight, rising again and again over the harrier while he, with superb side-slips, took evasive action at the last moment and easily avoided each lightning swoop of the falcon. All the time a continuous chattering and barking was kept up. At length, tiring of the sport—if sport it was—the peregrine made off, and the harrier flew away in the opposite direction. The flight of the harrier reminded my friend of the flight of a gull, but between the wing beats there were long graceful glides, during which the wing-tips were turned markedly up, the primaries well separated and showing light in between them, as in a soaring golden eagle.

On a morning recently, following on a violent gale from the north west, I saw a peregrine falcon come over, at a good height, and never have I seen a bird give a more vivid impression of speed. He—for it was a male bird—progressed in a series of dashes, so swift and impetuous that I thought at first he was in pursuit of prey. It may be that during those dashes he hoped to flush birds from beneath him but if so he was unsuccessful during the short time he was in my sight. That February gale was one of the most violent I have experienced. I happened to be at the time on upper Deeside and at the height of the storm my way took me through a wood of spruce. Trees were falling all around me—900 had fallen in a few hours—and it was remarkable to see how far trees could bend without being uprooted. During the fiercest gusts some of the spruces bent lower and lower until they were not far from the horizontal; with the temporary lessening of the wind they became more upright. No wonder, I thought, that trees should snap under so great a strain. The roar of the tempest in the wood was awe-inspiring; snow accompanied that storm and when the full moon rose into the cold, stern sky, frost accompanied the gale, which sent the snow drifting in great clouds over the moor. But in the old forest of Scots pines, trees which have seen the passing of centuries resisted that storm, and two days later, during a walk through a part of the old forest, I saw not a single blown tree.

In the Isle of Skye, so stormy was that winter (1942–3) the gale was scarcely noticed, but it browned and withered the flowers of the snow-drops so that, in exposed places, they were completely destroyed. I have not known this happen before.

None who loves our great Highland rivers—the Dee, the Spey, the Tay and others—can fail to have found pleasure in the oyster-catcher. Its deep red bill, ruby eye and handsome black and white plumage, its swift, steady flight and shrill whistle—these things make it an outstanding and very pleasant bird. Although oystercatchers are found on the Scottish coasts throughout the year it is probable that the winter birds are migrants from Scandinavia and Iceland. From September until earliest spring oystercatchers are no longer seen on the rivers of Scotland. It is a sign that the winter is trembling for its life when they first appear. They come in always from the sea—that is from the east—

and very gradually move up the rivers, knowing that the climate on the upper reaches is more severe than on the lower. On the lower shingle beds of the Dee, three or four miles above the tidal waters, they are first seen usually at the very end of February. In 1943 they were early. I happened to be passing a favourite haunt of theirs on the morning of February 18, and carefully watched for the oystercatchers, although I scarcely expected to see them then. But when I had almost given up hope of seeing my black and white friends a flock of them, standing close together on one of the lowest shingle beds of the Dee near Cults, caught my eye. From Aberdeen to Braemar is just under sixty miles by road, and rather more by the river. An oystercatcher could fly that distance comfortably in two hours, and yet a full month elapses between the arrival of the birds on the lower river and their appearance in the Braemar district. The birds had not been seen in the Balmoral district, ten miles east of Braemar, by March 6, though the weather from February 18 to March 6 had been spring-like. Observers at various points of a Highland river could do good work by compiling a chain of records on the arrival of the oystercatchers in their districts.

One of the most magnificent, as it is one of the rarest, British birds is the snowy owl. This great bird nests sparingly in the Arctic, and sometimes flies south to Scotland to winter there. A correspondent tells me that during the winter of 1927 a snowy owl, perhaps exhausted by its long overseas flight, took up its quarters beside a shepherd's house at Ramasaig on the western wing of the Isle of Skye. The snowy owl is easily recognised by its great size. It hunts by day rather than by night, and stoops at birds on the wing after the fashion of the peregrine falcon. At its nest, which is placed on the ground and which may contain as many as a dozen eggs, it is said to be very fierce, attacking a dog and even a man with ferocity.

As incubation begins when the first egg is laid, and as several days may elapse between the laying of each egg, eggs and well-grown young may be found together in the same nest of a snowy owl.

Sea birds—by sea birds I mean the true birds of ocean—have a mysterious sense which guides them unerringly over the vast ocean plain. R. M. Lockley in his book *Shearwaters*, which to my mind is one of the best bird books ever published, tells how by ringing he ascertained that some at all events of the shearwaters he marked on his island of Skokholm off the coast of Wales were in the habit of travelling backwards and forwards for food all the way to the Bay of Biscay. Each bird took a spell of several days on the egg, and it was during the time it was off duty that it made the long overseas journey. Mr. Lockley describes how a shearwater, taken from Skokholm by air to Venice and released there, returned safely to its mate, and wonders if that flight was made over the Alps, or over the vastly longer distance a sea route would entail. My own belief is that the whole of that great flight was made over the sea, for birds like the shearwater and gannet, which *never* fly over land of their own free will, are just as liable to become confused when they find themselves over land as a land bird when it finds itself over the sea. It is not long since I received news of a dead shearwater being found in one of the most inland districts of the Highlands—not far from the Perthshire Garry. That bird had undoubtedly been driven inland from the Atlantic by westerly storms and, weak and exhausted, had lost its bearings. Stormy petrels are frequently driven inland by storms and once they alight on land rarely seem to be able to make their way back to the ocean they unwillingly left.

A friend tells me of the curious taste of a pair of Orkney ravens. Over a Neolithic burial chamber at Westness, Rousay, a large cover house had been built. At one end of the building is an observation window, the plate glass held into the wooden frame by a thick bed of putty. A pair of ravens took a fancy to this putty and dug holes out of it, so that it had to be renewed more than once. When I was told this story it reminded me of the experience of a Highland deerstalker. His house is near a forest of old Scots pines, where crossbills have their home, and one spring a pair of these birds visited the skylight window of his house, and dug out, and apparently ate, the putty that held the window in position.

The only bird the raven fears on the ground is the golden eagle. A deerstalker once saw an eagle grasp in its great talons a raven which was disputing the eagle's right to feast on the carcase of a deer. The raven was instantly killed, strong bird though it was, by that deadly grip. When a sheep dies, gulls, hooded crows and ravens are attracted to the carcase. The greater black backed gull drives off other gulls, and also grey crows, from the sheep, but in its turn has to give precedence to the raven, and I have seen a greater black back standing respectfully by while a raven fed to repletion on the sheep's carcase.

The ravens repair their nest in February, but in the Scottish Highlands the eggs are not laid until March, although in the Border Country February is the laying month. Nesting as they do so early in the spring, when sleet, hail and snow may drive over their rock, the ravens are most careful to choose a sheltered nesting site. Almost always there is a projecting rock a little way above the nest, which acts as an 'eave' and keeps the sitting bird dry. The nest, too, is unusually deep—indeed so

The snow-capped Cairngorms. The north-facing corries of Braeriach in April.

Hard work on a warm Spring day. Harrowing by hand in the Western Isles.

Sowing and harrowing by hand. The boy pulls the harrow while his father broadcasts the oat seeds from a pail.

deep that it is sometimes impossible to see the eggs from above. It is warmly lined with wool and thus the five or six eggs, greenish in ground colour and heavily marked and spotted, are kept warm during the bird's absence. Ravens are conservative birds, very partial to an old nesting site, and although the young may be robbed or the eggs taken each year, they return again and again to their rock. But any unusual noise or disturbance in the neighbourhood is apt to scare them away. In the Isle of Skye during the reconstruction of a road a quarry was opened beneath a rock which was the nesting place of a pair of ravens. The birds became alarmed at the blasting in the quarry: they left the nest and although it is now six years ago since the quarry was in use they have not returned to the rock. It may be that this was the reason for the fights which I witnessed last spring between two pairs of ravens. The nesting places of these birds I did not locate, but furious fights continued until late in March, the birds flying at their topmost speed along the coast and with angry cries repeatedly diving to the attack.

Raven and eagle are often held up as admirable examples because they remain throughout life faithful to the same mate. But I believe that many other birds pair for life. I have little doubt that the red grouse and the ptarmigan do so, and it may be that even the smaller passerine birds, which collect into flocks in winter, and may leave this country separately for their winter quarters, when they return to their nesting site in spring, and find their mate at the old home, are faithful to the ties formed the season before and are happy in remembrance of their former happiness. But the raven, perhaps more than any bird I know, takes continued pleasure in the presence of its mate. Rare indeed is it to see a raven alone, even in the dead of winter. You may indeed see a solitary raven pass with steady, purposeful flight, and think him alone, but within a minute the form of his mate is seen, steering on the same course.

In the Western Highlands, where the relatively warm water of the Atlantic keeps the frost at bay, plant life is stirring in February. From the hazel trees of the glens catkins hang (in favourable seasons they are well grown before the end of January) and on sheltered banks early primroses open their yellow buds. Catkins of the hazel and birch appear long before there is any apparent stirring of the fast-closed leaf buds. In 1943, after a wet and stormy winter, we had, for the first time, a daffodil fully out on the last day of February. That early spring showed well the effect on the Scottish Highlands of an unusually prolonged spell of southwesterly weather—Atlantic weather it is sometimes called. From the Hebrides eastward to the hill country that is the backbone of Scotland the south west is a rain-laden wind, and week after week the west was drenched while the east Highlands enjoyed a long spell of mild, rainless weather. The result of this was that the plants which love sunshine and dryness were far forward in the east Highlands, but moisture-loving spring flowers were further back than in the wet and sunless west. For example, in the neighbourhood of Forres, one of the earliest districts, if not indeed the earliest, in Scotland, broom was coming into flower at the end of the month, at least twelve weeks earlier than its flowering time in Strathspey, and the winter wheat was covering the fields with a green carpet, yet the daffodils were later than in the west, where the prolonged rains of winter, and absence of frost, had brought them on before their time.

Were it possible to grow trees in the Hebrides and provide really good shelter, it is probable that certain semi-tropical plants would survive the winter. In another chapter I have recorded that hydrangeas in our garden in the treeless north west of Skye, in a most exposed situation, survive even a hard winter, and mesembryanthemums on a wall survive a mild winter. Our chief enemy is not frost but wind. It is impossible to grow salt-resisting firs such as *Pinus laricio* and *Pinus insignis* for a curious reason. Our ground is a rich loam, with a clay subsoil. During our rainy season, which is always accompanied by wind and lasts from October until March or even April, the soil becomes saturated, and because of the clay subsoil the water cannot drain away. The tap-root of the pine is unable to penetrate this clay sub-soil and the whole rooting system, being anchored in semi-liquid mud, 'gives', and the tree is blown down when only a few feet high. It may in its early years be held in place by stakes, but this artificial aid cannot be prolonged.

This adverse combination of wind, rain, and a hard clay 'pan' severely limits the choice of trees. After twelve years' experience, during which almost all the trees planted have failed, I have come to the conclusion that only surface-rooting trees are any good, and were I to plant again I would choose only the spruces—the Sitka or Menzies spruce and the Norwegian or common spruce. These, so far, have stood, but I suspect that when they reach any considerable height they will be overturned by some of our one hundred miles an hour winter gales.

When I mentioned that the pines were failures, I should perhaps have excepted the mountain pine of the prostrate variety (*Pinus montana pumilio*). This tree stands the gales moderately well, but it is of the bushy or prostrate form and none of them has reached a height of six feet in twelve years, although by spreading over the ground they have given a small amount of shelter.

We are in the curious position of having excellent soil, and yet being unable to take advantage of it. Our vegetable garden is perhaps the most exposed in the British Isles. It is on the 300 feet contour line, almost immediately above the sea, with no shelter from the prevailing west and south-west gales, although it is surrounded by a good stone wall six to eight feet high. To give one instance of the severity of our summer storms. In July, 1942, we had a row of dwarf peas with a magnificent show of flower. Successive gales swept the garden in August, and the young pods, and the plants which bore them, were shrivelled and blackened so that we did not have one dish of peas (or broad beans for that matter) that season.

Escallonia and veronica hedges give some shelter, but the storms which sweep past us even at mid-summer limit the speed of their growth. Carrots do well in the garden (but now the carrot fly has reached us), and so do strawberries, for the plants are low on the ground and they receive all the sun that shines. In other districts strawberry plants retain their leaves throughout the winter, but with us each leaf is blown away by the winter gales, and at the beginning of spring the plants appear lifeless, but later grow a complete new set of leaves.

Of late years the summers have certainly deteriorated. The weather broke on June 1st of the summer of 1942, and from then onwards, throughout summer, autumn, winter and the following spring there was no spell of settled weather. This sounds like an exaggeration, but as we keep an official meteorological record for the Air Ministry here we can check the weather of the past nine months. There was scarcely any summer in 1943 and fine spring days in 1944 were few and far between.

The wind died during the night. Heather fires that had glowed at dusk, fanned by strong gusts from the hills, gradually dimmed, flickered and were subdued by the dampness of the night air. Before sunrise chaffinch and thrush were in song; when the sun rose the air was at once warm and balmy as on a morning of June. Beside the river Dee, in the old garden of the manse of Crathie, many crocuses had opened their blue and yellow flowers and, although the month of March was but six days old, a wandering honey bee was gathering their pollen.

On the high moors at noon blue smoke was curling into the sunlit air from newly kindled fires. The heather, crisp and dry, was a warm reddish-brown in the strong light. Cock grouse, strong and lusty, with brilliant red combs, sprang crowing into the air, then sped above the moor in swift, rocking flight. On the west horizon rose in mystic beauty the Cairngorm range, the long summit ridge of Ben MacDhui white and shining and edged with black against the blue serene sky: near it stood Beinn Mheadhon of the great warts and Cairngorm itself. Singularly impressive did that great range seem when viewed on this brilliant day through an avenue of clear air between two heather fires.

At the side of the moorland track a mountain hare, still in its white winter coat, rose and fled away across the hillside, its snowy fur embarrassingly conspicuous to fox or eagle now that the last snow-drift had melted.

It seemed strange to traverse mile after mile of curlew country and neither to see nor hear one of these birds—for this day of almost summer warmth of early March had come while the curlew still lingered beside the shore, perhaps on the coast of Eire, perhaps even in France or Spain.

But later that month, on an evening when a cold breeze from the north had arisen after a quiet day, a bird-lover friend and I were in curlew country and listened to the low-toned liquid tremulous music of these long-billed birds which seems to embody the spirit of the wild moors and lonely, trackless places. The curlews' songs were short that evening, for the cold, dry air, blowing off Ben Vrackie freshly covered with snow, was not to their liking. The birds rose a little way in short flights, then quickly dropped into the sheltering heather as though glad to be out of that chill air. Had the evening been mild they would have remained longer in flight, and sung a longer song. Perhaps, too, they were a little tired, for the previous night an enemy raiding aeroplane had dropped a bomb at the edge of the moor, shattering the peace and quiet of that Highland strath and sending the curlew aloft to call wailingly and protestingly in their sorrow, so it seemed, at the folly of men.

But this evening the German raider stayed at home—or perhaps he was shot down by a British fighter before he could make his escape—the curlews were left in peace, and the old ravens that each night use a high rock here as a roosting place were undisturbed. We saw them flighting in after sunset.

All through the winter a considerable gathering of ravens had used the rock (to which I shall again refer in a succeeding chapter) each night as a roosting place, but now, at the end of March, most of the birds had apparently returned to their nesting sites. Some of those which remained may have been unmated birds; they came in singly, flying at a great height and croaking as they flew, their abrupt, barking cries loud and far-carrying. A colony of jackdaws were executing giddy aerial manœvres about the rock, calling the while with high-pitched calls, sharp and querulous, but the ravens kept aloof, for they roosted on one of the highest ledges. Swinging round with powerful, level flight as they prospected the land to see that no foe was near, those wandering viking ravens croaked and barked while a yellowhammer sang his simple song in a larch plantation far beneath them.

In the valley of the Tay, with its tributaries the Tummel and Garry, most of the larches are hybrids between the European larch and the Japanese larch. When leafless the Japanese larch may be identified by the rich brown colour of its branches. It buds early and is susceptible to frost, and it has been found that the hybrid between the two species combines, in that central Highland district, the two best qualities of both.

The previous day (March 25) I had seen my first wheatear—a rather early date for the Highlands of Scotland—and its arrival was at least a fortnight earlier than in the two previous cold springs of 1941 and 1942. Why is it that the male wheatear arrives always before his mate? The cock may be seen in Highland glens a week, even a fortnight, before he is joined by the less brightly plumaged hen. I like to think, and indeed it is probable, that he renews old loves and joys, and that the mate he finds on the boulder-strewn hillside is the same companion that shared his happiness the previous spring and summer. Were the wheatear a rarer species more would be thought of the beauty of the male.

I recently had the pleasure of watching on a Highland river a strangely plumaged oystercatcher. A friend of mine had written to tell me that it had returned for the seventh season in succession,[1] to its river haunts,

[1] It has again returned during the present spring of 1944.

and one spring morning of bright sunshine we set out to locate the bird. In the old forest (now, alas, being felled) a greater spotted woodpecker was hammering upon a tree, the noise resembling the blows of a riveter on the hull of some vessel under construction, although of course in a more subdued key. The lesser spotted woodpecker (a bird no larger than a chaffinch) is unknown in the Highlands but the greater spotted woodpecker is widely distributed, although nowhere common. The original Highland race became extinct more than a century ago but new arrivals have since populated many of the forests. To return to the oystercatcher. Everywhere we searched for him, without success, and were on the point of abandoning our quest when a fisherman told us that he had that morning seen the bird in a field. Here we found him feeding by himself a little apart from several paired birds. In the normal-plumaged oystercatcher the head, throat and back are jet-black. In this individual the head and throat are almost pure white, the white feathers extending a little way along the back. Round either eye is a circle of dark feathers. This considerable white area is faintly mottled with black.

At first sight the bird reminded me of a turnstone, though of course it is very much larger than that wader. After feeding upon worms for a time he took wing, flew across the river, and when at a considerable height changed the usual rapid wing beats to the slow, gull-like flaps that are associated with the song. From this I judged it to be a male. He has indeed been seen incubating the eggs, but both male and female undertake that task. Before we left the river we again saw the oystercatcher. He was then dozing on a stone on a shingle bed, his head tucked away beneath his feathers. He awoke and walked leisurely away, the sun shining on his ruby eye, his yellow bill and his white head. His mate had apparently not arrived, for he was all the time by himself. It is a sad commentary on the baseness of human instincts in some people that 'a man with a gun' should be after this beautiful and unusual bird. He has been warned off the estate, and it is to be hoped that his plans may miscarry and that this unusual oystercatcher may return for many more seasons to the shingle beds beside the swiftly flowing river where in spring birch and larch scent the air and the missel thrush from the highest trees sings his loud defiant song.

A correspondent who heard of this white-headed oystercatcher has written to me to say that several summers before, in Strathspey, he saw, among a flock of oystercatchers on the wing, a pure white individual. It may have been an albino, and albinos are, I believe, rarely fertile, but the oystercatcher I have described nests each season.[1]

[1] I have recently been sent a number of most interesting photographs of a pure white oystercatcher with his normally plumaged mate on a Highland river.

In March, and again in April, an immigration of redwings reaches the Hebrides. One morning the birds are seen on the whin bushes, on the walls, on the ground. At first glance they might be mistaken for thrushes, but their cinnamon flanks, and their white eye-stripes at once identify them. It is believed that these redwings are on passage to Iceland, and the Iceland redwing has now been separated from the Scandinavian redwing and is classed as a distinct species. I like to think, when I see them in the windswept treeless district of the north of Skye, that they will soon be singing in the stunted birch scrubs of Iceland, where the steam from boiling springs drifts slowly into the cool, clear air and on the horizon rise great hills covered with eternal snow and ice.

Writing of hot springs, I recall an amusing episode which occurred in Iceland when my friend and I were returning towards the coast after visiting the Great Geysir. We overtook a char-a-banc. Icelandic roads are not tarred, and the dust thrown up by that vehicle was almost suffocating. Mile after mile we drove in its wake, our driver constantly sounding his horn. The road was narrow, and the man at the wheel ahead of us did not, or perhaps would not, hear us. At length our driver could stand it no longer. He stopped the car, seized a stone from the road and threw it with all his might at the fast-retreating char-a-banc. His aim was naturally short, and having thus relieved his feelings he drove more slowly and was content to keep his station behind his rival.

It is always a heartening sign when the first solan—as the gannet is named in Scotland—swings with strong flight through the Minch. It was March 23 when I saw the first solan in the spring of 1943. Alasdair and I were setting small lines for codlings and flounders (haddock for some reason have been entirely absent from the Minch for two years now). The day, after months of wild weather, was calm and sunny. Beside a sunlit shore the lesser celandine had opened its yellow, shiny flowers, and primroses showed through the brown, matted grasses of the previous year. Setting a small line involves considerable labour. Lug-worms have to be dug in the sand at low tide, and in the Isle of Skye sandy shores are few and far between. After the worms have been dug several hundred hooks have to be baited; the boat must then be launched over a rough shingly shore and the line set about a quarter of a mile off-shore, preferably on a rising tide. The line may be lifted an hour after it has been set: I think a two-hour interval is best. If the line is left down too long dogfish, crabs and molluscs eat the fish off the hooks.

We returned after sunset to the shore. A strong, gusty wind, which brought with it the faint scent of burning heather, had suddenly sprung up from the east, buffeting the shags as they fought their way home to their roosting island. To lift the line under these conditions was no easy task, for the wind threatened to sweep the boat off its course as it was rowed slowly above the line, one of us rowing, the other lifting the hooks. From the darkening waters of the sea flounders and codlings gradually emerged and were hauled over the side until a fair-sized collection of fish lay at the bottom of the boat. It was a stiff row to the shore, for the wind was contrary and in the swell a landing was not too easy.

The month of March is the season for setting the great or long lines. These are set usually a mile or more off-shore, for cod, ling, hake, roker (a skate-like fish) and skate. Inside the three-mile limit, that is an imaginary line drawn three miles from land, no trawler is permitted to work. Even in peacetime it was difficult to keep trawlers from the prohibited area: in wartime they trawl where they like. It may be said that under these abnormal conditions it is their right to gather as much of the sea harvest as possible, but it is not generally realised that the deep-sea fish which enter the West Highland lochs and inshore waters in early spring come there for the purpose of spawning. Trawlers dragging their trawls backwards and forwards over the spawning beds destroy millions upon millions of ova and must seriously affect the future supply of fish. The local long-line fishermen are now afraid to set their lines, for they have learnt by experience that these are trawled up and destroyed during the hours of darkness—and under war conditions it is almost impossible to buy new lines or even second-hand ones.

I have mentioned that the first solan was seen on a sunny day of March. The previous year, at the same season, I had visited their great nesting haunt on Ailsa Craig, a bold, rocky isle which rises from the Firth of Clyde. Creag Ealasaid, or Ealasaid a' Chuain, Elizabeth of the Sea, that great rock was of old named in Gaelic. Even at a distance it is bold and massive; when one lands on its shore the cliffs give the impression of a vastness that is not exceeded by the precipices of St. Kilda, for its granite walls seem built to defy the storms of eternity. Raven and peregrine nest on Ailsa Craig, but it is the solan which attracts attention, because of the vast number of these birds which throng the ledges that rise, tier upon tier, to a height of almost 1000 feet. A babel of strident bird voices is constantly heard here from March until September. A little distance off the leeward side of the isle many soaring solans wheel and circle, the birds sailing at varying heights in the wind-eddy caused by the cliff. Others of the colony fly in from east or west with great bunches of seaweed for their nests or, later in the season, with fish for their young. On this particular visit, when we were approaching the Craig a solan flying near the boat suddenly checked its flight to make a quick surface dive, reappearing with a bunch of drifting seaweed in its bill. Instead of flying at once to its nesting ledge on the rock it made at least two more surface dives for seaweed, and did not fly to its nest until its bill was crammed full of the brown *fucus* weed.

On this visit I heard a strange story of a solan's revenge on a guillemot brooding beside it. The man who told me the tale was sitting one summer day at the top of the rock, and was amusing himself by throwing small stones at a solan on her nest far beneath him. After several stones had struck the bird it suddenly half-turned on the nest and struck its neighbour the guillemot, killing it instantly. The solan does not give the impression of great intelligence, and this individual evidently thought that the guillemot had been annoying it and must therefore die. Although the solan is not a clever bird it is a most skilled fisherman and a grand flier. On its fishing excursions over hundreds of miles of ocean it must see strange sights, these days of war—deadly missiles from flying boats dropping aslant upon lurking submarines, the swift wake of torpedoes speeding near the surface on their grim mission, derelict rafts, boats floating upturned, the bodies of the drowned—sorrowful sights for human eyes, but perhaps the solan is heedless of such things, for human affairs concern it not.

Culzean Castle, ancestral home of the Kennedies, stands on a rock beside the shore on the mainland over against Ailsa Craig, and as one sits at breakfast on a spring morning here one sees the solans passing a little way off-shore or diving in great numbers upon some herring shoal midway between the Ayrshire coast and the blue, snow-splashed hills of the Isle of Arran. The solan is almost always associated with a wild coast. Here, too, the outline is stern, but beauty is unexpectedly seen in the fields of golden daffodils which flower on the steep grassy slopes beneath the castle almost to the tide.

Near the castle is a small loch, sheltered by noble trees, where in the March air is the scent of resinous pines mingled with the perfume of the flowering currant. As I reached the loch I saw five swans swimming proudly and leisurely upon its sun-reflecting waters. Three of the five kept to themselves, and when these three birds approached me I could see the orange bills and erect necks which showed them to be whooper swans, winter visitors from Iceland. From the far end of the loch a golden-eye drake and three ducks now swam into view. Golden-eyes are usually timid birds, but these showed little fear and as the drake swam past, leading the quieter-plumaged ducks, I admired the lovely greenish sheen on his head and the white patch behind the eye which gives the species its name. The ducks swam in line, and at their passing a faint ripple spread slowly across the windless surface of the loch.

The male of the pair of mute swans which have their home on that loch resented the presence of the whooper swans, and in an attitude of defiance, with wings slightly raised and opened, swam arrogantly towards them when they approached. The whoopers retreated on these occasions, but they did so leisurely and without fear. When the mute swan drew near the whoopers it was interesting to notice his larger head and thicker and more arched neck.

In Iceland whoopers may sometimes be seen feeding on the grass, as geese do, a considerable distance from water. In Scotland they are almost always seen on the water, but I have more than once noticed them ashore feeding on the grass near the head of Loch Insh in Badenoch, a favourite winter and early spring haunt of the species.

In another chapter I have mentioned the habit of the buzzards of the Isle of Skye of perching upon telegraph posts. Only a few days ago I saw a bird on a perching place of this kind and attached to one leg was a rabbit snare, which did not seem to inconvenience the bird. Rabbits are the buzzard's chief food, and the noose may have become entangled in its foot while the bird was feeding on a snared rabbit. I chuckled to myself when an acquaintance rang me up one day, to tell me that he had seen three eagles perched on telegraph poles and that the royal birds had not troubled to fly away when his car had passed below them. I asked him if he was sure they were eagles: when he replied there was no doubt about it I had not the heart to disillusionise him and tell him they were of the species of the less noble buzzard. It is rarely a safe thing to say that a bird *never* does this or that—I remember Lord Grey of Fallodon saying that the only thing it was really safe to say was that the cock bird *never* laid the eggs —but I am fairly sure that the eagle does not perch on telegraph posts lining a main road, and am quite sure that *three* eagles would not have been seen perched thus in the same locality on the same day. This recollection of Lord Grey's remark recalls to my mind the occasion on which he acted as my chairman at a London lecture I gave in aid of some charity. I have done a good deal of lecturing in my time, but never have I had so admirable a chairman as Lord Grey. Combined with his deep love and knowledge of birds was a noble presence and clear, cultured voice. I remember that at the end of the lecture, when he made a few remarks, he was able to place his experiences against mine. Very few of

my chairmen have had sufficient knowledge of natural history to do that.
A joint lecture which Lord Grey and I gave to the English-Speaking
Union in Edinburgh was not without anxiety for me because of Lord
Grey's failing sight. Upwards of forty slides, from photographs which I
had taken, were shown of his waterfowl at Fallodon. There were three
of us on the platform. Lord Linlithgow (later Viceroy of India), Lord
Grey and myself. Because of his blindness Lord Grey could not see the
slides, and as he described each I had to point out the features of
interest. He had memorisèd the order in which the slides came, and he
told me that he would be 'done' if the operator got the order wrong.
Fortunately the lantern operator was an expert and no untoward
incident occurred, but I had moments of anxiety before the appearance
of each slide. I once showed my slides and a film in the state drawing
room of No. 10 Downing Street in aid of a charity. Ramsay MacDonald,
who was Prime Minister at the time, presided, coming straight from the
House of Commons, and made a very kind and friendly speech. Three
guineas were charged for seats, and the room was well filled. Those
days seem indeed remote at the present time.

The minister of a Methodist church permitted the sacred building to
be used for a lecture which I was giving to a local society. My
chairman, bluff, hearty and fond of good living, was in these unaccus-
tomed surroundings scarcely at his ease. His confusion was obvious
when, just as he rose to his feet to introduce the lecturer, the minister
in a strong, firm voice, told him, 'Be seated; we will now engage in
prayer.' My increasing deafness now makes it difficult for me to hear
conversation or my chairman's remarks—although a greater loss to me
is the fact that unaided I now can hear no bird song—and thus arose an
embarrassing incident when I was lecturing to a church society in a
church hall. It had been arranged that a well-known piper should play a
tune after the chairman's remarks. The piper was a friend of mine, and
at the suitable moment I was to call upon him. But unknown to me the
chairman, his address ended, called on a member of the audience to
engage in prayer. Before he could comply, in all innocence I rose to my
feet, and in a loud voice called for a tune. I noticed that there was a
certain embarrassment visible, but it was not until afterwards that I
knew what I had done, for the piper at once rose and played of his best.
I told the story later to Lord Lang, then Archbishop of Canterbury, and
he said with a chuckle, 'Did the piper win?' But an even better story
was told me by a friend, of a Highland concert at which the chairman
proclaimed that the proceedings were to be opened by pipe music
played by a certain piper. Now the skill of this piper was not rated too

highly locally, and he had scarcely taken the pipes from their box and walked on to the platform when one of the audience with more vigour than taste, yelled at the top of his voice 'Sit doon, ye ——'. At once the chairman was on his feet and called out in stern and disapproving tones, 'Who called the piper a ——?' Came the answer instantly, in the broadest Scots, 'Fa caa'd (Who called) the —— a *piper*?'

To be asked to lecture before the Royal Institution in London is, perhaps, the highest honour which can be paid to a lecturer. There he has an hour—lectures are strictly limited to an hour—of pure pleasure, for he is speaking to a cultured and intelligent audience in an admirably appointed lecture theatre with a first-class lantern and a skilled operator. Twenty years ago, when first I lectured at the Royal Institution, it was the custom to ring a bell at the end of the hour, and to keep on ringing it until the lecturer took the hint, but this practice has now been abandoned although it is still an unwritten law—and a very good one too—that no lecture should exceed the hour. I have had the privilege of giving a good many addresses before the Royal Institution, and I look back upon each one of them with pleasure. The last occasion was in the late spring of 1942 when thousands of tulips were in flower in St. James's Park and I was impressed by the fragrance of their scent, for I do not remember having noticed this scent before. In Kew azalea and rhododendron were a blaze of colour and it was all very peaceful, so that it was difficult to realise that the world's greatest war was then being waged.

March is the month when raven and eagle nest. On March 15 of the year 1943 I had the interesting experience of seeing within a couple of miles of one another a raven and an eagle at their nests. The morning had been one of rain and tempest, but the afternoon was fair, although a stiff breeze continued to blow. While I was still some distance from the ravine where a pair of ravens each year rear their brood I saw the male flying low over the moor. The sitting bird must have been keeping a sharp lookout, for the instant I came in sight of the nest she flew off, but instead of flying agitatedly backwards and forwards as usual rose rapidly on the strong breeze and, flying at a considerable height, time after time turned upon her back, to fly for a second or two in that position. The movements of turning on her back, and of righting herself again, were made so swiftly that the human eye could scarcely follow them. On this day the joy of being borne upward by the rising wind current overmastered any anxiety she may have felt for the safety of her eggs.

This pair of ravens use the same nest each year. The cup is so deep that even when looking across the gully it is impossible to see the eggs. The gully is interesting, for here rock doves may always be found during the nesting season and it is the only inland site in Skye where I have known these coast-dwellers to nest.

The hills that afternoon ran water, yet for a few hours the rain held off, and I continued on my way to a high rock where each year a pair of eagles have their eyrie. I did not expect to find the eagle brooding— the season was a fortnight too early for that—but I thought that I might have the pleasure of seeing her and her mate performing some of those fine aerial evolutions which I had watched in previous seasons. Before I had reached the cliff I saw the pair of golden plover which each spring nest in an area of moderately dry ground rise near me and fly, close together, across the hill. There was no sign of the eagles on the face of the cliff, but when I came in sight of the eyrie I was glad to see the great bird rise from the nest and fly, as is her custom, silently away. From the cliff top it is possible to see the eyrie, but not the eggs, and so I had no means of discovering whether the eggs, or the first egg (for there is an interval of several days between the laying of the first egg and the second), had actually been laid. I have never known an eagle lay as early as March 15, although an eyrie which I used to visit in a fir tree in the central High-lands usually had eggs around the 20th of that month.[1] The eagle is not dependent, to the same degree as most birds, upon weather conditions for her nesting, for her food is equally plentiful—or the reverse—in severe weather as in spring-like conditions. But at times heavy snow-falls in late March and April force the eagle to desert her eggs. A good many years ago I visited an eyrie in a high-lying and exposed gully after a spring snowfall of unusual depth. The only black object in all that snowy expanse was the eagle. She had not yet laid her first egg, but was brooding in order to keep the eyrie free of snow. The golden eagle pairs for life and a West Highland deerstalker told me recently a story which illustrates the eagle's faithfulness to his mate, and to her memory. Four years ago a heavy snowstorm drifted up a golden eagle's eyrie shortly after the female bird had begun to sit. For two days the eggs were hidden in the snow; at the end of that time the eagle was able to brood them once more, not knowing that the embryos had been killed by exposure. All through April and May she continued to brood the frosted eggs. In June she still brooded, but as there was no possibility of the eggs hatching, and the eagle had become very thin, the stalker re-moved the eggs. He was doubtful if she would survive, and when, later

[1] In 1944 I heard of an eaglet hatched in an eyrie by April 15—an exceptionally early date.

in the season, he found a dead eagle on the ground he was fairly certain that this was the same bird.

The sequel is interesting. Each spring the male eagle has built up the eyrie, but has not taken another mate, although that eyrie is at the heart of golden eagle country and it is inconceivable that the widowed eagle would have had any difficulty in finding another mate had he had a mind to do so. To birds, death is a mystery, but one of which they have no fear, and I am sure that when death claims a bird's mate the survivor does not realise that there is a finality in the parting. This eagle is awaiting his mate's return, and is keeping the home in repair against that return. When he sails above the high tops, or alights upon some sharp summit or narrow ridge his eye searches the far horizons. On lonely flights his keen eyes watch for that small dark speck that would cheer his heart, for he would know that at last his mate was returning to him and that he would no longer live alone. But he looks in vain, and his sharp yelping cry, echoing through the corries, is unanswered.

Prolonged rough weather, such as we endured in the spring of 1943, has the effect of retarding the nesting of many of the smaller birds. That cheery pest the house sparrow begins to build in February if the weather be calm. But that year the birds in the last week of March—and even a week later—were still going in flocks, wild as at mid-winter. Skylarks arrive at the exposed and wind-swept district of northern Skye early in February. That year, two months later, they were still in flocks and flew restlessly above the wind-beaten grasses. Wind is distasteful to most birds, and their lot that spring was not a pleasant one. One afternoon in March, after weeks of continuous gales and heavy winds, I found many skylarks sheltering on the leeward side of a rounded hill, very wet and clothed with grass and short heather. I doubt whether a single lark would have been there had the weather been more pleasant. Sea birds, too, suffered from the violence of the storms. I had sent me a ring taken from the leg of what the finder described as a large 'buzzard-like bird' washed up on the shore of the Skye coast at Tallisker, some forty miles from where we live. On the ring was the following inscription 'MUS. NAT. REYKJAVIK ICELAND 3/2065'. The ring was sent to the British Museum (Natural History), enquiries were set on foot, and it was found that the bird was a great skua, a bird of the year, ringed on 2nd August, 1942, at Kvisker on the south-east coast of Iceland, between the ice-cap and the sea. The great skua is a bold, fierce bird. A friend of mine shot a teal; before he could pick it up a great skua had swooped down and begun to tear the duck to pieces.

When the rain in sheets sweeps over the sodden land and the south-west wind shakes the houses and breaks the crocuses which, obeying the impulse of a mild temperature, thrust their flower spikes into the sombre air, many earthworms may be seen crawling forlornly over the grass and over the road. They have been flooded out of their homes by the water: when they crawl out on to a road they seem to lose their way, become inert and die, being unable, when above ground, to withstand the onslaught of wind and rain. The herring gulls know that food in plenty awaits them on a day of this kind: they may be seen quartering the ground carefully (for the strong head wind enables them to cover an area at scarcely more than walking speed), every now and again suddenly checking their flight and dropping to earth to pick up a worm.

In most districts rooks follow the plough. On the north-west wing of the Isle of Skye herring gulls take their place. These birds roost, and have their nests, on the islets of the Minch, and each morning before sunrise fly in to the fields of Skye, where they are ready for the early worm on the grass fields, and are in ample time to finish their breakfast before the arrival of the ploughman, who is rarely an early riser in Skye.

Towards the end of March a new arrival joins the herring gulls behind the plough. This is the lesser black backed gull, which is a summer visitor to the coasts of Scotland and the Isles. These handsome birds with slate-grey backs have reached us from the sunnier coasts of Spain and Africa where they have passed the winter months.

Of late years a distinction has been made by ornithologists between the British lesser black backed gull and the Scandinavian lesser black back, the distinction being that the British gull's mantle is slate-grey, and its Scandinavian cousin's mantle is black.

The effect of prolonged Atlantic storms is most pronounced on islands which are exposed to the action of wind and sea. Towards the end of March I accompanied the lobster fishermen to Fladday Chuain island group, a cluster of islands rising from the waters of the Minch about five miles off the north-west coast of Skye. Here the scene was almost lifeless. The slopes of the islands had been scored and washed by rain and salt spray until in places the grass had almost disappeared. Rabbits and sheep had died or were dying, and there were fewer barnacle geese than usual. There was bright sunshine, but a strong, hard wind from the east was blowing and there were rainbow colours on the flying crests of the waves. A pair of ravens each March nest on the island known as Guala Mhór (Big Shoulder) and the mate of the sitting bird was searching for food, or nesting material, on the main island.

Bare and lifeless did the isles seem in the hard sunshine and it was not easy to realise that spring was nominally at hand, and that two months later the grass would be fresh and green after the healing breath of spring had touched it.

In the third week of March, when the wind for a time had gone to rest, my wife that spring heard the dainty high-pitched song of the golden-crested wren coming from a small plantation of Sitka spruces below our house, the only trees of any height in the district. All the sparrows and starlings of the neighbourhood infest this very small plantation and the sparrows make their untidy nests in the trees. I saw the gold-crest that afternoon, flitting about among the trees as it fed on insects. It was evidently on migration, for it was neither heard nor seen again.

At the end of the month a gaggle of white-fronted geese passed over the house. We do not often see these geese, and they were flying not toward the north, as might have been expected at that season, but south, in the teeth of a heavy wind which made even slow progress difficult.

The fairy-like grace and beauty of the Common Gull.

On the Western Camp, one of the grandest spots. "East of Wallula," rising

'*Fitheach moch, feannag, anmoch.* The raven (in voice) early,
the hooded crow late'—a sign of fair weather.

OLD CELTIC SAYING

In the Highlands the birth of spring is slow. Rain and wind,
cold mist driven before the storm, hail and even snow may
be the lot of the unhappy animals (man included) in this
month. Wind is disliked by birds even more than rain or
snow and thus at the close of the rugged, grim and stormy
April of 1943 the green plover of Skye had not hatched
their eggs and even the hardy sparrows had not laid.

Perhaps not within living memory was there so remarkable an April.
Along the western seaboard and in the Hebrides it was the worst April
for many a long year: in the Central Highlands it was one of the best
Aprils during the last quarter of a century. In April there is usually a
spell of east or north-east wind which brings fine weather to the west,
but in 1943 the wind was almost continuously from the south west—
always a wet wind in the west and usually a dry one in the Central Highlands. In the Isle of Skye, after a fortnight which might have been
December, when the young buds on tree and hedge were withered and
scorched as though twenty degrees of frost had burnt out their life, and
when the petals of the daffodils were torn into shreds or lay prostrate on
the grass, unrecognisable except for their colour, the sun rose bright on
April 15 and for a brief interval the gale subsided. That morning the
whin bushes near our house erupted redwings. They perched on the
topmost spikes or flitted among the undergrowth as they rested and fed
awhile before continuing their migration to Scandinavia, or it may be to
Iceland. Where a narrow road passes through the whins I saw ahead of
me the flash of white as a male Greenland wheatear rose. Across to
some closely grazed grassland he flew, then a second bird took wing and
followed him. The sight of those wheatears cheered me, for I knew
that, despite the rain-laden gales which had swept over land and sea, the
season of good weather was surely advancing. The Greenland wheatear
is rather larger in size than the British wheatear, and the under parts in
the male are of a deeper buff. The species breeds in Iceland, Greenland
and Labrador, and crosses the British Isles on migration both in spring
and autumn. The Greenland wheatear has the unusual habit of perching
upon trees during its migration, for the common wheatear never
perches on anything higher than a wall.

During a visit to the Central Highlands in April I noticed that the common wheatear here was less numerous than farther west where, next to the meadow pipit, it is perhaps the most characteristic bird of the stone-strewn common grazing lands. In the old natural-sown pine forests of the Central Highlands I saw crossbills and bull-finches. At the edge of the forest, at a height of perhaps 1500 feet, a bullfinch rose from the heather and flew down the hill, to disappear in the nearest tree. I followed it, and saw that it was a male in all the rich beauty of the spring plumage. His black head, in which were set bright beady black eyes, full of intelligence, his breast and flanks glowing with the pink flush of a summer sunrise, his soft, slate-grey back, the black wings and tail—all harmonised in a lovely colour scheme that was warm and gay against the cold green of the pine needles, and the white grass and brown heather beyond. For a time the bullfinch remained almost motionless, then flew across to a birch tree, where he perched and seemed to doze. There I left him, with the blue smoke of a heather fire rising into the air on the farther side of the glen, beneath wreaths of the winter snow.

During my stay in the Central Highlands I was fishing the upper waters of the Dee when I saw approaching me down-stream, and flying perhaps thirty feet above the river, a large bird of black plumage which at first glance seemed entirely strange. Surely, I thought, this cannot be a cormorant, sixty miles and more from the sea! The bird passed, and then I saw that it was a male capercaillie, perhaps alarmed by the tree-felling which is now, alas, taking place everywhere in the Highlands, and seeking less disturbed quarters. I have elsewhere mentioned the effect of the denudation of the forests on their bird residents.

This passing mention of a cormorant calls to my mind an anecdote a friend of mine told me about this voracious bird. The cormorant is hated on a river because of the number of salmon parr it devours. It takes not only these small fish but frequently swallows a large sea trout and on one occasion Angus MacPherson of Invershin[1] took from the gullet of a cormorant he had shot a grilse of between five and six pounds. The story my friend told me is as follows: A cormorant was fast asleep on a rock beside a Highland river. My friend and a second angler were passing that way and one of them said to the other, 'A pity I have no gun.' 'Never mind the gun,' replied the second, 'I will get the

[1] Angus is perhaps the most skilled fisherman on the Shin. To watch him throw a fly or play a salmon is to see an expert at work.

bird without that.' He was carrying a stout hazel stick at the time, and at once set out to stalk his quarry. The cormorant slept soundly, and my friend was able to approach without awakening it, and struck it cleanly on the head with his stick, killing it instantly. It was found to have been digesting a large brown trout.

The heron is not so voracious a feeder as the cormorant, but kills many young fish and is therefore looked upon with disfavour and sometimes shot on certain Highland rivers. A heron shot on the Lax-ford river on 10th October 1941 had an aluminium ring bearing the number 6178 and the words 'University Oslo' on one of its legs. I sent the ring to the Bird-Ringing Committee of the British Museum and, after making enquiries they reported to me that this bird had been ringed as a nestling near Egersund, South-west Norway on June 12, 1941. It is good to think that even a world-war has been unable entirely to bring to a standstill such peaceful occupations as bird ringing in an enemy-occupied country.

A bird which cheers the angler in April on a Highland river is the graceful grey wagtail. Its long tail, artistic flight and soft yellow plumage ('grey wagtail', like 'oystercatcher' and certain other birds' names, is a misnomer) as it flits airily over some deep rocky pool dis-tract the angler's thoughts from the serious business of fishing. There was no greater bird lover than Edward Grey of Fallodon, and an anec-dote told me by his Highland gillie is worth recording. Lord Grey used to fish the Cassley in April, staying in rooms at the post office at Rose-hall. One year a pair of grey wagtails began to make their nest in a rock above one of the best pools of the river. When Lord Grey saw the wagtails at work as he fished the top of the pool he said to his fisherman: 'We must leave this pool, for if we remain on it there is a risk that the wagtails may forsake their nest.' From that day onwards, until the end of his time on the river, Edward Grey could not be persuaded to throw a line on this pool although, as his fisherman told me afterwards, there was a certainty that he would have caught salmon there. Lord Grey was a good salmon fisherman, but an even better trout fisherman. On one occasion when I was staying at Chillingham Castle (in the park near the castle is the famous herd of Chillingham cattle which have an ancestry of at least a thousand years) and was going on to stay at Fallodon, Edward Grey had been fishing a trout stream near, and called for me in his car. His blindness was then increasing, yet he had caught a basket of good trout which gave him satisfaction, so that he did not mind the drenching he had received from the rain and sleet of that bitter spring day. That was the charm of the man: he had a deep love for the simple things—the curlew-haunted moors which rose to the west of Fallodon with cloud-capped Cheviot on the horizon, the duck which came wild to his sanctuary in autumn and by spring had completely lost their fear, the seals of the Farnes, the missel thrushes and blackbirds of his own woods. His sight had almost gone when the fulmar began to form nesting colonies on the seacliffs in the neighbourhood of Fallodon, and it was a bitter thing to him that he could not see their forms, nor the grace and poetry of their flight. He remarked that if I told him a gannet was passing, or some other seabird that he knew of old, he could visualise it, but the fulmar was unknown to him and thus he was unable to form a mental picture of the bird. I had perhaps a greater understanding of what he was feeling because of my own increasing deafness which prevented me from hearing the songs of birds that formerly I knew so well.

The most handsome duck of the Highland rivers is the goosander. It is the largest British duck, a skilled diver and a voracious feeder on small fish, and therefore on Highland lochs and rivers a price is often set on its head. It is now found nesting throughout the Highlands of Scotland, but was formerly a bird of the high north, and it was not until 1871 that the first nest was found in Britain. During the winter of 1875-1876 there was a large immigration of goosanders from the far north, and that spring many of them remained in Scotland to nest. The species now breeds in the counties of Sutherland, Ross, Inverness, Nairn, Aberdeen, and Perth. It has of late been found nesting in the shires of Selkirk and Dumfries. I have never seen the nest in the Outer or Inner Hebrides, where its place is taken by the smaller red-breasted merganser. In the drake goosander the bottle-green head, white breast, the flanks lovely with a salmon-pink flush, the black back—these colours blend to a strikingly handsome plumage. The bill is long, with serrated teeth, and is blood red.

The usual nesting place of the goosander is an old hollow in fir or alder growing near a swift river or burn. The young when hatched are armed with long claws, and are able to climb up the smooth inside walls of the hollow until, on reaching the entrance, they fall without harm to the ground outside. They are then led by the duck (the drakes usually join into flocks and take no further part in the proceedings) to the river or hill burn, where they are immediately at home in the water, passing unharmed down formidable rapids. When alarmed they scatter at once and hide under the banks.

I was recently on the hills and was approaching a Highland loch which lies at a height of 2600 feet above sea level. A pair of goosanders passed me, flying fast from the pine-clothed glen far below. They were evidently flying up to the loch on a fishing expedition but the unexpected appearance of man in that lonely country caused them to change their plans. They flew on beyond the loch, swung abruptly round over a snow-covered boulder-strewn slope beyond it, then returned at the same fast pace over my head, as they descended toward the glen whence they had come. I thought to myself that I had unwittingly saved the lives of a number of the loch's trout that morning.

A pair of goosanders met disaster in an unoccupied stalking lodge standing beside a loch. Since the species nests in hollow trees it is possible that the chimneys of the lodge offered attractions as a nesting site. My friend who told me the story said that on entering the lodge in the spring (it had been empty all winter) he heard a hoarse quacking and saw a large bird shuffling and skidding round the corner of a passage. The goosander (for such it was) was chased from room to room, and was at last persuaded to leave by the front door. It made at once for the loch, diving immediately and remaining long submerged. Its mate was found dead in the chimney.

The eagle has repaired her eyrie during March, and has perhaps laid her two speckled, rounded eggs before that month was out. All through April (for her incubation period is six weeks) she broods her eggs and exceptionally, if she be an early nester, hatches her two eaglets before the end of the month. In the West Highlands the eagle nests in a rock: in the Central Highlands in a tree or a rock. I visited recently an ancestral nesting site, for the time being (I hope the birds may return) unoccupied. It is in a very old Scots pine on the slopes of a hill. The tree stands alone, in an exposed site, and the gales it has withstood, and which have sent many trees crashing to earth, have blown sticks from the eyrie and have scattered them on the heather below. The eagle chooses as a nesting site a tree, or rock which provides a good 'take-off'. The ground falls sharply away below most eyries, so that the great bird, on springing from the nest, may fill her wings with the breeze.

When I found this eyrie unoccupied I walked, keeping to the highest fringe of the forest, to a rock a few miles away where for many years a pair of eagles have nested. The sun was bright but a cold wind blew off the snow-covered hills and a sudden hailstorm for a time whitened the heather. One of the eagles I soon saw ahead of me. He (for I think from the size it was the male) was being mobbed by two grey crows. Ignoring them, he rose to a great height then, half closing his wings, planed westward at a great speed. Through the trees below me a herd of stags moved quickly: chaffinches sang from the old pines and a pair of cross-bills flew past. The eyrie I did not see. The old eyries were that spring unoccupied, but I heard a rumour that the birds were nesting on a high rock near.

A stalker once saw a fox in full chase after a hare. He then saw that an eagle had noticed the fox, and had swooped down low over the animal. The fox, upset by this unexpected attack, gave up the chase, and the eagle then sailed away. That hare ought to have been grateful to the eagle for saving its life.

On a rocky hill-face a colony of jackdaws nest. One day a great commotion was seen among the colony. A golden eagle had appeared and was sailing backwards and forwards across the face of the rock, ignoring the furious attacks of the jackdaws. The eagle alighted, then rose and swooped down to the foot of the rock, where it picked up a rabbit. At least three times it dropped the rabbit from a considerable height, and the observer who told me the story thought that it did this in order to kill the animal. At length, bearing its prey, the eagle set out in the direction of its eyrie some distance away.

The head deerstalker of a West Highland forest was out one late summer day looking for a woodcock for the pot. He was crossing rocky ground on which there was some natural wood when he heard an unearthly yell followed almost at once by a second scream. Thinking the cries were human he hurried as fast as he could to a cliff less than 100 yards below him and when he was half-way to the rock saw a golden eagle rise from the ground, then dive earthward once more. Almost immediately two more blood-curdling yells shattered the silence, and when he had reached the edge of the cliff he saw below him a wild goat standing on her hind legs and bravely defending her little kid about two days old. The small creature had the intelligence to keep between its mother's hind legs when the eagle stooped and was thus protected from the fierce and determined attacks. The stalker watched the great eagle thrice swoop down upon the kid, then he showed himself and the eagle flew away.

The eagle, as I have earlier mentioned, is frequently mistaken for the buzzard, and indeed when seen at a distance it is sometimes difficult to distinguish the species. A near view at once settles the identity of the bird. One of the differences between the two species in flight is that the eagle's primaries are turned up when soaring, not so the buzzard's. The buzzard often hovers, kestrel-like, but the eagle never hovers.

In mid-April the sandpiper arrives at the Highland rivers and lochs where it will nest in May. This charming wader is found beside almost every burn; the highest nesting place that I know is on a small loch 2600 feet above the sea. As it stands on some boulder or runs daintily along at the water's margin the sandpiper bobs not only its short tail but the whole of the hinder part of its body with a wagtail-like motion.

The sandpiper's flight is distinctive. It moves, at no great speed, low over the water with vibrating wing beats, then glides to its favourite perch, where it sometimes holds for a second, its wings outstretched above it in the form of a V.

Sandpipers at times perch on trees, especially when they are anxious about their young concealed among the grass in the vicinity. They seem, like the oystercatcher, to ascend the rivers from the coast, arriving on the lower reaches a good deal earlier than on the upper. In the Inner Hebrides they sometimes nest at the estuary of a small burn within a hundred yards of the open sea, and it is interesting that they arrive here considerably later than on the east coast rivers.

The sandpiper has a very wide nesting range. In Europe it is found in summer in Norway, Finland and northern Russia; in the south it nests in Portugal, central Spain, the south of France, central Italy, the Balkan peninsula, Crimea and Caucasia. In Asia it is found nesting in Persia, Afghanistan, Kashmir and Tibet, and east to China and Japan. In Africa it has nested in Uganda and Kenya.

At the beginning of this chapter I mentioned that a cormorant had once been killed with a grilse in its gullet. Reptilian in appearance, the cormorant yet responds to love's impulse in the spring. On an afternoon of sunshine a friend and I were beside a fresh-water loch much frequented by the species before the birds make for their nesting colonies up and down the coast. That sunny afternoon we had seen more than twenty cormorants in the air together above the loch. Two birds separated from the flock and for the best part of half an hour flew backwards and forwards overhead. They kept very close together, and all the time gained height until they were perhaps 4000 feet above us and scarcely visible to the unaided eye. They then began to slant earthward at great speed as a peregrine falcon might do, but soon checked their descent and continued their courtship flight. Where we stood the sun had already set, but still shone on the cormorants, and the white thigh spots on both birds were visible. I had never before seen cormorants rise so high nor remain so long in the air, all the while urging themselves forward at their topmost speed. At last they disappeared, still travelling at a great height, towards a neighbouring loch.

In most Highland districts the corncrake arrives during the last week in April. This furtive bird of the rich earth-red plumage is so clumsy in flight, and so reluctant to take wing, it seems incredible that it should make a double flight each year across hundreds of miles of ocean. When it arrives it seems to have had quite enough of aerial travelling, and during the summer months it is no easy matter to make a corncrake rise from the ground.

A sudden alarm may cause it to take wing. A few days ago I saw a man running (to keep himself warm, for the day was bitter) across a field of young rye grass, not very long but sufficiently dense to conceal a corncrake. He was half-way across when he almost trod on one of these birds. The surprise was mutual and the landrail, taking precipitate flight, blundered against a fence, falling dazed to the ground. In a moment, to my relief, it was up again, and running like a rodent for the shelter of some small trees. Judging from the harsh sounds which have since come from the same field, it is none the worse, and the pair have been seen engaged in courtship.

During the last thirty years the corncrake has decreased throughout England, Wales and the mainland of Scotland. Only in the western and northern islands off the Scottish coast, and in the west of Ireland, has there been no appreciable diminution in its numbers. It is generally supposed by those who have studied the question that the corncrake's enemy has been the reaping machine. So long as the cutting of the rye grass and meadow hay was done by the scythe the sitting corncrake had time to leave her eggs, or to move her young, before the danger was upon her. But the reaping machine travels many times faster than the scythe and often decapitates the brooding bird or her young. This theory is supported by the fact that the districts where the bird is still holding its own are those where grass and corn are reaped by the sickle and not, unless exceptionally, by the reaper.

The corncrake is a late nester, and eggs are found in July, and even in August. They number from 6 to 14, and there are records of 18 and 19 in the same nest, though here it is probable that two females laid together. They hatch quickly, in rather more than a fortnight, and the young are able to run about actively from the first day of their hatching. They can fly at the age of 34 days but are not fully feathered until 7 or 8 weeks.

This bird with the deceptively slovenly flight migrates far south at the end of the summer, and winters in Africa, Arabia and Madagascar. Toward the north it is found nesting in The Faeroes, Norway, Sweden and north Russia, but is not apparently found in Iceland.

It is in April that the males of the black grouse indulge most vigorously in their tourneys at dawn. The male black grouse is termed the black-cock. Each morning, except in heavy rain or snow, from December until June, blackcock are accustomed to resort to the same little knoll, there to display and spar one with another until sunrise. This display comes primarily no doubt from a love impulse, but it is indulged in even when no greyhen (as the female of the species is called) is in sight to spur on the combatants with her presence. The male is at any time a bold and handsome bird with his glossy black plumage, white wing bar and red wattle above the eye. In the display the tail is spread, the wings are partly drooped and the red wattle above the eye distended. The white under tail-coverts are spread wide and prominently displayed, and it is these alone which sometimes attract the human eye in the half light of early morning. But it is more often than not the song of the blackcock that first draws attention to the 'lek' or gathering. The sound is a musical bubbling, not unlike the cooing of a pigeon. Selous, who made a special study of the courtship, describes it as beginning with the cooing notes 'rōo, rōo, rōo' or 'krōo, krōo, krōo', followed by sounds which suggested to his mind a sentence of human speech. During this crooning the head and neck are thrust forward and the neck is distended. When two opponents face one another they stand erect, dancing on their feet like trained boxers, then rush in and strike at one another with their feet, leaping and sometimes half flying a little way into the air, at the same time uttering a loud and sharp 'tchū-whai', a wheezing, sneezing sound. I have more than once known a blackcock fly on to the roof of the hide in which I was observing and photographing the display and the cooing song, eager and quickly repeated, when heard immediately above my head was very loud. On the knoll, clothed with short heather and much trampled by the birds, I watched the blackcock creeping low over the ground, and could see their throats vibrate with their cries. Each new arrival flying in added to the excitement. At intervals the birds seemed to grow tired of their ardour, but it took little to set them going once again although I never saw them display once the sun's rays had touched the fighting ground. My observations were made mostly in May and June, but one frosty morning of December when I visited the knoll and concealed myself beside it I found that even at this season the 'lek' was held, for one blackcock after another flew in to display as the dawn strengthened and its cold light replaced that of the moon.

Birds and animals have come to realise that a railway train is more harmless to them than a man. From a railway carriage window I have several times seen blackcock displaying at their fighting ground near the line. There is the classic example of an oystercatcher which nested between the metals of the main line of the Highland Railway, and it is an everyday occurrence to see stags and hinds grazing beside a railway which passes through their forest. If the train should stop the animals become suspicious: if a passenger should alight they at once take to their heels. Birds nesting beside a road often show the same fearlessness of motor cars. When passing along the shore of some West Highland sea loch I have sometimes seen an oystercatcher brooding on her eggs. If I kept moving (although I might slow down the car to a walking pace) the bird was not alarmed, but the moment I stopped the car and showed myself she jumped up and ran furtively away.

Flowers of the Highlands are slow in venturing abroad, for they know that winter may return in April and even in May. The most characteristic spring flower of the Highland hills is the purple mountain saxifrage. It is a hardy plant, and, unlike most early flowers prefers a northern sunless exposure. Its buds, and the flowers when first they open, are rose-coloured but later are inclined to purple although I think the plant would be more aptly named the rosy mountain saxifrage. It is fond of limestone and basaltic formations and is not at home on granite—that is why it is almost absent from the Cairngorm area. Its flowers add a touch of warm colour to the stark and grim precipices of Beinn Storr and to the shattered and splintered ridges of the Cuillin in the Isle of Skye.

When I hear of some old castle lived in for a thousand years by the same family I sometimes wonder whether a pair of golden eagles might not claim that their ancestors in a direct line had nested in the same site for an equal number of years. Birds, fortunately or unfortunately, keep no family records, are the owners of no family tree, so we shall never be able to solve this mystery.

The golden eagle is perhaps longest-lived among birds. There is the record of a golden eagle that was shot in France: engraved on a gold collar round its neck was its name (it had evidently been used in falconry), its native country, and a date 95 years earlier. Most of the Gaelic place-names in the Highlands are very old. On maps of the Scottish hills and glens will be found a number of place-names 'Creag na h- Iolaire', the translation of which is 'The Eagle's Rock'. This Celtic name persists in districts where, at the present day, Gaelic is no longer a living language. In certain of these 'Eagle's Rocks' the golden eagle still has its eyrie. There are others where the birds are no longer to be found, but one such rock which I never thought would see an eagle again has in recent years been once more occupied by a pair of these grand birds, perhaps the descendants of the pair which gave their name to the rock. Later in this chapter I shall write a more detailed account of this nesting place.

As a boy I used, forty years ago (in and around the year 1903), to watch a pair of golden eagles at their eyrie on a certain rock. Now, in the summer of 1943, they are still nesting on the rock. Another eyrie, which to my knowledge has been tenanted regularly during the past thirty-seven years, is in a native Scots pine growing in a high glen almost 2000 ft. above the sea in the Central Highlands. When first I knew that eyrie it was three or four feet deep and was built three quarters of the way up the tree. When I visited it last, in the early summer of 1943, it reached the tree top and the latest nest was actually the highest part of the tree. The whole structure now had the appearance of a number of wicker baskets piled one on top of the other, not quite, but almost vertically, and was approximately fifteen feet high. The pine is an old one— perhaps 300 years—and each spring it must bear an increased weight, which may now exceed a ton.

Golden eagles' eyries in trees are sometimes blown down by winter gales and the wonder is that this does not happen more frequently, for the tree chosen is almost always an outlying one on an exposed hillside, where, as I have earlier mentioned, no neighbouring trees impede the eagle in her 'take-off' from the nest. One pair of eagles for a number of seasons nested in a birch tree. In 1943 I visited their glen for the first time for twenty-nine years. The birch, gnarled and solitary, was still there, but the eyrie had fallen.

Ptarmigan are conservative birds in their habits, returning to the same 'territory' each spring on a high pass, or in some rock-strewn corrie. On the morning of May 28, 1943, I passed a stony knoll at the edge of a snowfield where on May 27, 1903—forty years ago, almost to a day—I had, as a boy, found with much enthusiasm my first ptarmigan's nest. I had not been on that ground for many years, nor was I thinking of those early times when, from the very same knoll, a cock ptarmigan rose into the air and showed by his behaviour that he had a sitting mate near. I have little doubt that this was a descendant of the pair which had tenanted the knoll forty years before. But I found that the stock of ptarmigan had greatly decreased since then. Whereas in those days I was accustomed to see twenty or thirty pairs of ptarmigan on this ground during a day's walk I now found only two pairs. There was evidence that foxes were plentiful, and during the present war-days so many stalkers and keepers are serving in the army that, as I have elsewhere mentioned in this book, the fox has increased alarmingly throughout the Highlands, killing grouse and ptarmigan and, more important, large numbers of lambs. Hybrids between ptarmigan and red grouse are very rare, but a deerstalker on a Highland forest told me that on one occasion he found a ptarmigan had paired with a grouse: he saw both birds at the nest so there was no doubt of the identification.

The oystercatcher is not generally reckoned as a long-lived bird but my wife and I have known a small shingly shore at the margin of a sea loch in the Isle of Skye where a pair of oystercatchers have nested since the year 1926, when first we visited the district. The war makes travelling difficult. Instead of using one's own car, and being able to stop when one likes, one is now fortunate in being able to squeeze into a public service vehicle. Travelling in the local bus, we passed that shingle bed early on a May morning of 1943 and saw that the 'change-over' between the male and female of this pair of oystercatchers was at that moment actually in progress.

In these grim days of war there is the danger that we may lose some of our rarer birds, ancient tenants of immemorial trees. I have mentioned that much of the old indigenous pine forest has been, or is being felled, so that the birds have had to seek fresh quarters. Deer forests are changing hands and new keepers and stalkers are being brought to them. In one forest where the eagle has always been protected I hear a report, which I hope is exaggerated, of a new keeper waging war on these noble birds. Even in time of peace, such things are difficult to prevent; how much harder must this be in the midst of war!

Mock battles with live ammunition are being fought on Highland hills. An eagle sailing lazily offers a tempting target, and a ptarmigan is a welcome addition to one's rations.

I have elsewhere mentioned that the whooper swan occasionally nests in the Highlands of Scotland, choosing an island on an unfrequented loch, high up among the hills and perhaps 2000 feet and more above the sea.

The whooper's eggs, being rare, are much prized by collectors. A certain remote loch, on an island of which a pair of whooper swans were nesting, was carefully guarded by a watcher, day and night, during the nesting season. One dark night the watcher heard a commotion out on the loch. The disturbance grew louder and from the darkness there emerged a dripping figure, a box slung over his naked shoulder. 'Ah ha!' said the watcher, 'I have you, my man; now let me see those swan's eggs which you have in that box.' The dripping figure sadly shook his head. 'Yes!' he said 'you have caught me, right enough; I suppose that I shall have to hand over the eggs to you.' He opened the box, and gave three swan's eggs to the watcher, who, naturally elated, returned them later to the nest. In due time the eggs hatched and the cygnets swam proudly on the loch after the old birds. But as time passed it was seen that those cygnets differed subtly from their supposed parents, and finally there could be no doubt about it—they were young *mute swans*. The collector had had a false bottom made to his box; had taken out mute swan's eggs to the island; had placed the whooper's eggs in the false bottom when he robbed the nest, and, in case he was caught on his return, had placed the mute swan's eggs at the top of the box!

This at least is the story which I had from a friend and of which I am reminded each time I look at the picture on the wall of my study of the pair of whoopers at their island home in the heart of the Highlands.

Ravens are long-lived birds and like the eagle return each year to the same nesting rock. Since in most districts they are unwelcome and are shot or trapped it is rare for them to continue unmolested their tenancy over a long number of years.

At the close of the nesting season all the ravens of a district often roost together on some ledge of a high rock and toward sunset may be seen winging their way from every direction to that rock. In winter the Highland ravens are reinforced by visitors from the north east—from Norway, Finland, Lapland and perhaps Russia. There is a rock in the Pitlochry district of Perthshire on the property of my friend Commander Edmund Fergusson, a bird lover and keen naturalist, where considerable numbers of ravens roost during the winter months. In that district the raven is scarce as a nesting species, and I think that the birds are immigrants, like the London-roosting starlings in winter. Highland ravens nest in early March, yet in 1943 these roosting birds tenanted the rock, coming in each night to roost, until far beyond that time. Indeed their numbers considerably increased during April. On April 18, Commander Fergusson counted forty ravens, *in pairs*, flying in to roost. He wrote to me again in May, for as late as the 2nd of that month he had counted over forty ravens flighting to their ledge. Scottish ravens by that time had well-grown young, and my friend had begun to think that this raven colony might consist of non-breeding birds, when, the very next night, he found the rock deserted. The birds had gone for another season. The inference is, I think, that these were ravens which nest very far north, in country which would lie under snow until May. It is indeed possible that the rock may lie in the track of migrating ravens, and that during April it may be used as a halting place by birds on passage before taking off on their flight across the North Sea. I do not think that a community of paired ravens so late in the spring has hitherto been recorded in the British Isles and no raven nests in, or near this particular cliff. The previous two winters the birds had left the district much earlier in the spring.

Sea birds nest usually in colonies and the same cliffs are in use which have been tenanted for centuries. On Boreray, near St. Kilda, gannets in thousands nest where they nested at the time of Martin Martin's visit in the year 1690. Like the eagle the gannet matures slowly and does not nest until it is four years old; it can therefore be inferred that it is a long-lived bird, but we have no means as yet of knowing the length of the gannet's natural life.

Kittiwakes return year after year to the same cliff or rocky island. The birds may have tenanted the cliff for many centuries. On a summer evening, toward sunset, they wheel delicately above the cliff, their white plumage rose-tinted by the last rays of the sun. The sea laps at the base of the rock; every now and then there is a sighing as the ocean swell flows slowly and mightily over the cliff foot. The sea thrift is rosy on the ledges; red and brown seaweed clothes the lower rocks left bare by the ebbing tide. Who would think, to see these graceful, affectionate birds at their nests, that they had spent (as they are known to spend) their winter at the very heart of the Atlantic, more than a thousand miles from land. In size and appearance the kittiwake resembles the common gull, and yet how different are their habits when the nesting season has ended. The common gull keeps to the coast throughout the autumn and winter and even upon occasion flies inland: the kittiwake moves out into the Atlantic, feeding and sleeping on the sea, and has reached mid-ocean by the end of September or the early part of October.

As is well known submarine activity in this war has been at its fiercest in mid-Atlantic. The oil floating in this area must be a deadly menace to bird life, and the kittiwake would be one of the chief sufferers. During the nesting season of 1943 I visited three kittiwake colonies in the Isle of Skye. Two were entirely deserted; the third had only a small proportion of its usual population. It is of course not possible to say with certainty that this was due to the oil menace but it looked very like it.

The air was fresh and clean in Glen Quoich after a night of rain. Across the valley of the Dee Morrone towered; on the south-east horizon the cone of Lochnagar rose to a sombre sky. The Quoich flowed clear, though in great volume, through the glen of immemorial pines and stirred the Devil's Punch-bowl at Allanquoich. In Gaelic Glen Quoich is Gleann Cuach, Glen of the *Cuach* or Drinking-cup; it may have received its name from the cup-worn rocks (of which the Devil's Punch-bowl is one) in which the Quoich Water whirls and eddies.

I followed an old track that climbed toward the north out of the pines. This track ends at a peat moss near the summit of Carn Elrig Mór, a name which seems to commemorate the hunting of deer in olden days. It may be a hundred years since the people of the district used the moss, for there is now little evidence of the peat banks. I thought if the old folk who toiled up to that high moss to 'cast peats' (as the Mar saying has it) could have forseen the present nightmare days they would have devoutly thanked Heaven that they lived in a happier era. Yet in the midst of war the view was calm and peaceful. West rose the Cairngorms in clear sunlight. Strong and full of beauty was this high hill range. The great snowfield upon Monadh Mór curled over like a wave about to break. There was much snow also in the Soldier's Corrie of Cairntoul. When viewed either from the east or from the west Cairntoul is the most picturesque of the Cairngorms. It is not huge or rounded like Ben MacDhui or Braeriach: from the east it is seen to rise as it were delicately, with an attractive crater-shaped corrie that reaches almost to the summit. When seen from Lairig Ghru to the north of it Cairntoul is bold and stern, and is sharp-pointed like a height of the western seaboard. Nearer to me, and rising from the farther side of Glen Quoich, was Beinn a' Bhuird, flooded with soft, clear sunlight. At the edge of the forest I saw signs of the fury of the past winter's storms. The gales which had uprooted hundreds of planted trees in the lower glens and valleys had failed to master the old native pines, yet great limbs had been wrenched from them and lay, still fresh and green, on the heather below. Delicate moths fluttered above this heather, emphasising the peace and serenity which had succeeded the wild weather of winter and early spring. Here and there the dwarf birch (betula nana) held its characteristic rounded, short-stalked leaves a foot or more above the ground. High overhead an eagle made his un-hurried way westward, almost touching the fringe of a thunder cloud from which the sun appeared and for a while shone with tropical heat. Then the sky darkened. Mist dropped to the level summit of Beinn a' Bhuird and the great rocks so recently bathed in sunlight were now in an austere twilight.

I thought of an early summer day in a fir-clad Highland glen when Dara the collie and I had sat awhile beneath one of its oldest trees. A goosander that day made her aerial way quietly up the glen, rising and falling with an easy, gliding flight. Her nesting recess I saw later; it was in an ancient pine, bleached, hollow and lifeless, and the entrance to the hole—goosander's down gave away the nesting place—was perhaps twelve feet from the ground. A tree pipit made aerial excursions that day and sang his simple song as he sailed daintily down to his favourite branch.

Near where I sat was the pine in which a pair of golden eagles had nested to my knowledge for the better part of half a century. A cuckoo with gliding flight flew past me up the glen and settled, swaying, on the bleached branch of a neighbouring dead tree, looking intently around her. She was, I think, searching for the nest of the tree pipit that had been singing near.

The Cuckoo's Storm and the Lapwing's Storm are local names for a proverbial cold snap early in May, yet it is rare for the ground to be more deeply snow-covered in May than at any time during the preceding winter. This happened in May, 1943. On the north-west seaboard of Skye the morning of May 9 was fine, calm and sunny. In the afternoon heavy hail began to fall, and, being followed by still heavier snow, at

A Cormorant Colony.

A Guillemot Colony— one is seen holding a fish.

Razorbills: a kittiwake is passing them in flight.

nine o'clock in the evening the ground was hidden below a uniform fall of three inches.

The warmth of the previous morning had hastened the growth of the grass: when the hail began to fall there was a scent of a new-mown lawn in the air, for the hail was bruising the young grass and causing its perfume to escape. In great flakes the snow fell all that evening, and when I went out at sunset I saw a thrush perched dazedly on a small ash (the only tree in the garden). It had a brood of full-grown young ones, and all food supply for itself and its brood was cut off. It now stood, quite still and silent, as though stupefied. When the snow ceased that night there was heard no voice of bird—the profound stillness and silence was broken by no sound save the subdued roar, now ebbing, now flowing, of the swell on the shore. The mist was low, but through the cloud-curtain could be seen the snowy hills of Uist, Harris and Lewis. Even the lesser isles of the Minch—Iasgair, Fladday Chuain, Bord Cruinn or the Round Table where MacDonald of old hid his title deeds—were sprinkled with snow as a cake is sprinkled with sugar. In sunshine next morning the snowy landscape was dazzling, yet even the strong midday sun did not melt the snow.

But that May snowfall in Skye was as nothing compared to the severity of the same storm in the Central and Eastern Highlands. On the high moors of Balmoral and Braemar grouse had nested early, for the spring had been unusually mild. A day or two before the storm broke grouse's nests were filled with ten, eleven, and even twelve eggs, on which the hen grouse were brooding closely. All Saturday and Sunday the snow fell steadily, and was driven into deep wreaths by a fierce north wind. On the Monday morning a crust had been formed sufficiently firm to bear the weight of a man. The grouse had been driven from their eggs or had been buried deeply where they sat. Some of the birds returned to their nests after the snow melted, but the embryos within the eggs had been killed and thus in a brief space the hopes of a record season were blighted.

Certain of the high-growing birches in full leaf had been twisted and crushed by the weight of snow. The havoc wrought among the young of curlew, oystercatcher, lapwing and other birds was great. Sandpipers almost disappeared from certain Highland districts. The young birch leaves in the track of the frost-laden wind were shrivelled and exposed; larch woods on the high hill faces seemed as though a forest fire had passed through them. Roads were blocked and cars abandoned. Lambs, sheep and, on one farm of Upper Donside, a number of cattle perished in the blinding drift. Had it not been for the war, much would have been written of that storm of snow which, for the second week of

May, was probably the most severe in living memory in the Scottish Highlands; indeed as late as July some of the drifts were still unmelted on the high hills.

Fruit crops were in a night ruined. A friend of mine was lamenting that she would be quite unable to cope with the black currant crop in her garden, so laden were the bushes. The frost which succeeded the snow before sunrise killed each blossom, and neither in that, nor in any other garden of the district, was there a single currant to pull.

May sees the unfolding of many of the wild plants and wild flowers of the Highlands. The yellow, labiate flowers of the trefoil may cover some wind-swept hill slope with gold, and among them may be admired the prostrate flower-spikes of the milkwort, laden with small blossoms of a deep and radiant blue. In the Western Highlands and Inner Hebrides the wild hyacinth crowns in glory many a small field which the scientific farmer would say could be improved (and the wild hyacinth eliminated) by the application of some fertiliser. I think that the most dense canopy of wild hyacinths I ever saw was in a field at Lochbuie in the Isle of Mull. During a period of dark and mist-laden days I often had occasion to pass the field, and the glory of that blue canopy seemed the greater under those sombre conditions. Perhaps one in five hundred wild hyacinths are white; like white heather they are more plentiful in some places than in others.

The marsh marigold flowers as a rule early in May, and usually well before the wild hyacinth. But in this year of 1943 things were topsy-turvy and marsh marigolds were still in blossom a week after the Longest Day, when most of the wild hyacinths had long formed their fruit. In the Central Highlands the wild hyacinth is less common than farther west. Along the valley of the Aberdeenshire Dee I have never found it: when planted there in gardens it grows, but does not seem to spread.

Earlier in this chapter I mentioned briefly the prevalence of a place-name which showed that certain rocks in the Highlands were of old tenanted by eagles. In a western glen is a rock which bears the place-name Creag na h- Iolaire, the Eagle's Rock. For long the rock was empty, then one season the King of Birds returned to the rock and brought his Queen with him.

It was evening when, after a long walk through the hills, I came in sight of the Eagle's Rock. Three eaglets had been hatched in the eyrie, and I learned that this particular eagle had laid three eggs, and had hatched and reared three young, during each of the six preceding years.

On the occasion of my visit I found that she had again hatched three eaglets, but one of them lay dead at the edge of the nest: it had probably been pecked to death by the survivors. During early life golden eaglets are most pugnacious. I have watched one eaglet daily attack the other, hammering it unmercifully on the head, neck and back, so that it barely escaped with its life, and have no doubt that the weaker bird is on occasion actually killed.

Around the two surviving eaglets a feast of food was spread—six mountain hares and two grouse. Although the eaglets were still in white down and had not grown their feathers, one of them was already fierce and advanced without hesitation to the attack, waddling across the eyrie and opening wide its beak in defiance. The parent eagles had brought to the eyrie several green-leaved rowan branches, freshly torn from some distant tree.

Perhaps twenty-five yards from the eyrie was a large boulder, half-embedded in the heather of the steep hillside. This was evidently used by the eagles as a site on which to disembowel their prey, for upon it were scattered the entrails and legs of many hares, some fresh, others old and dried.

My companion told me that this pair of eagles fed almost entirely on hares, but that on one occasion the previous year he had seen no fewer than seven grey crows, all neatly skinned, in the eyrie. Since the grey crow is the arch-enemy of the game preserver, the killing of these pests by the eagle should be a mark in its favour.

The eagle had left the eyrie, and now gave a fine display of soaring. Higher and higher she rose, leaning on the wind, until she disappeared over the summit of a neighbouring hill. Her mate had by now joined her, and before they vanished the two sailed in wide spirals. From the hillside opposite I saw her return, but before this I watched a battle in the eyrie, one eaglet attacking the other and driving it from the nest on to the ledge. Here it had room to conceal itself, for the ledge was a broad one, and in places wild hyacinths were in flower upon it; below the eyrie oak ferns grew amongst the rocks.

Although in the Central Highlands the majority of eagles' eyries are robbed each year, the birds find sanctuary farther west. I heard a report in May 1943 that a pair of eagles had arrived at a high cliff where previously the species was unknown.[1] At first I suspected that in this instance buzzard and eagle were being confused, but on my second visit to the cliff I had the good fortune to have an excellent and pro-longed view of one of the birds. The day was brilliantly fine and the sky

[1] They were still in the neighbourhood in May 1944 but so far as is known did not nest.

cloudless, and after I had sat awhile on a sunny slope facing the cliff I saw an eagle sail out of the shade into the sunlight. After a time it planed swiftly to a grassy hillside, where it alighted and made a leisurely toilet: it obligingly spread its tail so that I was able to see that the base was white. This denoted an immature bird, perhaps in its second or third year.

When the eagle rose and began to fly in the direction of the cliff all the birds of the air seemed to mob it. First to swoop were a pair of ravens; then a pair of kestrels took up the attack, and finally a buzzard. The eagle with a sudden characteristic motion of one wing easily eluded its tormentors, but the buzzard caused it to turn on its back, displaying its talons to the attacking bird. When the eagle disappeared from my view a good mile distant one of the kestrels was still swooping repeatedly at it with undiminished fury.

The northward surge of bird migration is late in reaching the Highlands. A few swallows[1] and sandmartins arrive in April, but the majority of these birds wisely delay their coming until May. It is indeed often mid-May or even later before house martins and swifts reach their haunts in the Highlands.

Few birds are happy in a rainy climate. It is no doubt because of the heavy rainfall that the swallow tribe is less numerous in the West Highlands than in Central and Eastern districts of Scotland. The swift, although this bird is not one of the swallow tribe but has nearer affinity with the nightjar, does not, so far as I am aware, nest in any West Highland district. It is absent from Oban, from Mallaig, from Kyle of Lochalsh, from Skye. It is seen in late May and early June flying north east, doubtless on passage to nesting haunts in Norway, and again in August or September during the southward migration, but it does not nest with us although in the west insect life is abundant and indeed more plentiful than in the Central Highlands. The swift likes to keep its feathers dry, and who can blame it? The swift is perhaps the only summer migrant equally at home in a lonely shooting lodge as in a village, town or city. It is pleasant to watch swifts circling high above the traffic-thronged streets of Edinburgh and Glasgow, for they nest in the heart of these cities, and indeed in each city, town and village of Scotland, except, as I have said, in the Western Highlands. Tomintoul and Braemar are reckoned to be the two highest villages in Scotland. They stand a full 1100 feet above the sea and both have a considerable swift population. I happened to pass through Tomintoul on a dark misty morning early in summer. It was not long after sunrise and still

[1] In 1944 I saw the first swallow in Skye on May 6.

A pair of Great Skuas on Unst.

A Razorbill at home.

On the Cairngorms.

Looking from Monadh Mór across to Braeriach in early June.

grey. The swifts were reluctantly bestirring themselves and were flying from their snug quarters beneath the eaves of the houses into the damp ungenial air. The cloud ceiling was low, and as the birds flew backwards and forwards beneath it they looked rather larger than their true size. Later in the summer I was waiting for the bus at Braemar to convey me a few miles down the Dee valley. The bus, which starts from the Fife Arms Hotel, was late, and I had ample opportunity of watching the swifts and house martins which were nesting on the hotel. I can recall only one other house in the Highlands which provides nesting sites for so many of these birds—and that is Ceannacroc shooting lodge, standing by itself far up Glen Moriston. Both these buildings are high, but five miles or so above Braemar I watched a pair of swifts entering and leaving their nesting hole in the outbuilding of a crofter's cottage at Inverey no more than nine feet above the ground.

House martins are at times even later than swifts in arriving at their nesting sites. It is frequently mid-summer when they begin to build their mud nests and if a dry, hot spell is then experienced they may have difficulty in continuing the work.

This happened in the summer of 1943. At one of the houses of the small township of Inverey house martins for the first time had arrived that summer, and when I visited the place two pairs of these gentle and attractive birds had half-built their nests beneath the eaves. The weather for some days had been unusually hot and dry and the mud which the birds had been using had now dried, nor indeed was there moist earth to be seen anywhere in the neighbourhood.

Thus the martins were of necessity idle: they flew backwards and forwards high in the brilliant blue sky above the house, from time to time entering their unfinished nests and resting awhile in them. In the evening, when the soft sun lit up the snowfields high on the Cairngorms, the birds from their mud-houses carried on a continuous twittering and singing. A pail filled with earth moistened to the consistency of mud was spread on the roadway below the house in the hopes that the birds would notice and use it, but they preferred to wait for broken weather, and, as I heard later, did not rear their young until September, at the end of which month the first snowfall of winter came to the Cairngorms. Before the martins were astir next morning I left the place, shrouded in a thick, cold mist.

Like the swifts and martins the tern family are late in arriving at their nesting haunts. Terns are mainly salt-water birds. Neither the Sandwich nor the roseate tern can be said to be a Highland-nesting species, and of the remaining three—the common tern, the Arctic tern and the lesser tern—the common tern is the only one that is reckoned to nest beside fresh water, although without actually shooting the bird—a horrible practice—it is sometimes difficult to distinguish between the common and the Arctic species. Along the rivers Spey and Dee the common tern nests (not in colonies as on the coast, but sparingly as single pairs, widely spaced) right up to the high reaches. On the river A'an, a tributary of the Spey, with its source near the summit of Ben MacDhui, Scotland's second highest hill, I saw terns hovering at a height of almost 1400 feet above the sea, and was assured that they nested there. I had only a fleeting view of one bird so was unable to identify the species, although it was clearly either a common or an Arctic tern.

It was a grey, misty day when I crossed from Braemar to the A'an valley, and when I approached Inchrory lodge I saw ahead of me a blaze of colour on a little knoll. It was as if here, and here only, an invisible sun shone. When I neared the place I saw that a rock garden more lovely than any I had yet looked upon had been made since my last visit. The reds of various species of *silenes*, the snowy whites of the saxifrages, the pale yellow of *dryas octopetala*—these and many other Alpine plants formed a dense carpet of bloom as unexpected as it was delightful to see. The limestone of the A'an valley is specially favourable to lowly plants of the hills, and the result of care, knowledge and assiduity in so favourable an environment has been a rock garden of singular beauty.

But to return to the sea swallows, as the terns are often called because of their swallow-like tails and graceful flight. When they reach us in May they have flown far. Swallow, swift and house martin have travelled, perhaps from South Africa—a long journey but nothing like so far as that undertaken by the Arctic tern. Like the great shearwater, the Arctic tern[1] travels each season from the Southern Hemisphere to the Northern in the spring to nest, and in autumn, after the nesting season is over, from the Northern Hemisphere back to the Southern, there to pass our winter season, which is the Antarctic summer. To account for this tremendous journey it might perhaps be suggested that the fish of tropic seas do not suit the terns. But in that event could the birds not remain off the coast of southern Europe where the winter season is temperate, and where our native population of fish-loving gannets make their winter home? It seems that, like many of its human friends (who,

[1] All arctic terns do not travel thus far, but some of them are believed to make this great journey.

alas, are usually unable to gratify this desire) the Arctic tern prefers to follow summer from one hemisphere to the other. It is known that the great shearwater—a more powerful bird than the tern, and of swifter flight—after its nesting season on Tristan da Cunha travels north, passes as quickly as possible through the seas of the tropical zone (since life there is presumably distasteful to it) and is found on the Newfoundland Banks in our northern summer, which is its winter.

Could the Arctic tern and the great shearwater describe their experiences on these vast flights they might unfold a tale of entrancing interest. The Arctic tern nests much farther north than Scotland, and I have seen its eggs in the low ice-fringed shore of northern Spitsbergen. From the lesser icebergs of that snowy archipelago to the great icebergs of the Antarctic is a journey of almost fantastic length. It must take months of flying, but the tern, unlike the swallow, is at home on the sea, although it rarely alights on the water, but rests upon floating wreckage, which these war-time days must be all too plentiful. I imagine that heavy seas would be distasteful, if not indeed fatal to it, and that during a storm it must keep on the wing except for very brief rests. Its flight is wandering and apparently inconsequent, yet in its head it carries a compass so accurate that for many weeks it travels unerringly toward the south until at last it flies beneath the midnight sun in the keen air of the Antarctic and sees its goal, the white-sheeted hills where the snowy petrel breeds and the low ice-margined shores where penguins bow and court.

There can have been few Mays more beautiful than that of the tragic year 1940, when our armies were being swept backward by an avalanche of tanks and men to the beaches of Dunkirk. At this time fell two Highland officers who could ill be spared from their native land—Captain Ian Matheson, Scots Guards, and Viscount Fincastle, Cameron Highlanders. Both were great friends of ours, and were lovers of the hills and glens and of the people who lived in these glens. Both were good pipers, and were loved by their men. In those early, unprepared days they gave their lives for the things they held most dear. In their loss is seen clearly the tragedy and futility of war, which mows down the flower of manhood of all nations.

June is the crowning glory of the Highland year. There is no darkness between sunset and sunrise; land and sea are bathed in a mystic twilight when the hard outline of the material world is softened and behind the veil is sensed the realm of spiritual beauty. The high corries of the hills become fresh and green; in the glens the heavy-foliaged birches drench the air with perfume. The bird chorus is scarcely so loud as in May, but when the air is sweet after rain and the winds are at rest during the early part of the month there is as yet no lessening in the beauty of the dawn chorus.

I associate early days of June, overflowing with beauty, with that strange inscrutable bird the red throated diver. This summer visitor, larger than a duck but smaller than a goose, frequents some of the more lonely and smaller lochs of the West Highlands, and of an evening flies down from its remote hill loch to fish in the sea. It lays its two large eggs, of a dark brown ground colour and heavily mottled with a still darker shade, at the very edge of the water, so that the bird when she leaves them is able to dive straight into and below the water, noiselessly and with scarcely a ripple.

I was crossing the hills of a Hebridean island one June day. A white mist hung close upon these hills from its birthplace over the Atlantic: the mist sent out aerial billows that broke with clammy breath upon the lower slopes. The sea mist and the hill mist had not united; between the two was a zone of clear although overcast weather. As I walked through this cloud-free zone I saw ahead of me a lochan reflecting in its glassy surface the grey unbroken canopy of cloud which hung almost motionless a few hundred feet above it.

On a low promontory I saw the snake-like head and neck of a bird of considerable size; as I looked they seemed stealthily to withdraw into the coarse grasses and become one with them. I stood still, and after a time the head reappeared and as the neck was cautiously raised the pale greyness of the feathers and the strong bill, slightly upturned at the tip, told me that this was a red throated diver, evidently brooding her eggs.

The following morning, at the beginning of a long walk across the hills, I passed the lochan. The mist had evaporated from the ocean and had gone from the hills, and now the June sun shone from a cloud-dappled fine-weather sky upon the hill tarn. Through my glass I could see from a distance the diver on her nest but as I walked nearer I noticed that the bird, unseen by me, must have submerged, for a diver, very much on the alert, was now swimming quietly on the peat-stained water. The bird dived often, each time reappearing on the surface at a different part of the lochan, and in order that the period of her suspense should be shortened I walked quickly to the nesting place. Judge my surprise, then, to see the brooding diver rise from her eggs almost at my feet and dive with scarcely a ripple; the bird I had seen on the water was her mate, who had perhaps come to take his turn on the eggs.

In the nesting hollow lay two large brown eggs. I left the tarn at once, for I knew that the red throated diver is a temperamental bird and readily forsakes her eggs. But I had time to notice, as the pair swam close together, that the bird which had been sitting was clearly smaller than the bird on guard, and that the brick-red throat was less brightly coloured.

Late that night, after a twelve-hour walk I came again in sight of the tarn shortly before sunset. This time there was only one diver at the nesting site—the more brightly plumaged of the two birds. He was floating quietly upon the water and as I watched him through a stalking glass from a distance he carefully cleaned and oiled his feathers, time and again moistening his bill, then touching his back with it and with a swift movement rubbing the back of his head over his back, to spread the oil over the plumage. His feathers oiled and preened to his satis-faction he lay on his side on the water and oiled his white under-plumage, rapidly shaking one leg in the air as he did so. This done, he stood up or raised himself on the water, beating his wings, and a few seconds later, as an afterthought, shaking his absurdly short tail. At last he dived, reappeared on the surface, dived again, then swam fast towards the nest. I thought to see him climb laboriously on to the eggs, but he swam out into the lochan and there made a second and equally elabo-rate toilet. This done, he became suddenly alert, rose from the water, and on quickly driven wings flew fast toward the invisible Atlantic a thousand feet below him, there, no doubt to begin his evening fishing. The red throated diver during the nesting season fishes usually in salt water, although there may be fresh-water lochs containing trout in the neighbourhood. But the black throated diver fishes mainly in fresh water.

The evening was warm, and there was no likelihood of the eggs taking harm during his absence. He may have known that his mate was due to relieve him, for a few minutes later as I was continuing my home-ward walk I saw a diver flying in fast from the direction of the sea, and climbing in long zig-zags in order to gain height. I pictured her arriving above the tarn, planing down and alighting with a rush on the quiet water, to climb a little later on to the low promontory and brood her two eggs during the soft twilight of a perfect June night, when the hills and moors are dew-drenched and refreshed after the heat of the day.

The flight of the red throated diver is characteristic: it is fast and straight, and the long neck is held slightly curved. Because the wings are narrow and the tail so short as to be almost non-existent the diver is unable to soar but must always drive its wings fast. Thus the flight from the Atlantic to a loch 1000 feet above sea level must entail considerable exertion: this flight the bird makes at least twice a day after fishing. The downward flight is relatively easy, but when the diver has fished well and has swallowed perhaps a dozen young coal-fish that thousand-foot climb must be arduous. It might be thought that the red throated diver would prefer to avoid that vertical flight and, whenever possible, would fish for trout in a neighbouring hill loch of the same or nearly the same elevation, yet almost always it seeks the sea. Fishermen, when they feel inclined to shoot this bird because of its fancied depredations among their trout, should therefore remember that it prefers salt-water fish to fresh. Indeed, after the nesting season the diver makes its home entirely on the sea until the following summer, in winter ranging south to the Mediterranean and the Black Sea. In summer it is found nesting very far north. I have seen the nest no more than 500 miles from the North Pole, at the edge of the ice on a low island where skulls and bones of walruses lay around the nesting site, at the edge of a brackish lagoon.

Scarcely an early summer passes without the recording of an osprey 'recovered' on some Highland moor. The bird which has been found is usually sent to the local taxidermist, a paragraph appears in the press, and then the matter is forgotten and there is one less of these beautiful and rare birds in Europe. When and where was the last nest of the osprey in the Scottish Highlands? Until the close of the last century a pair nested in the ruined castle upon the island of Loch an Eilein in Rothiemurchus. On a small isle on Loch Arkaig in Lochaber a second pair, being most carefully protected by the Lochiel family, nested for a few years longer. Mr. Murdo Matheson, a keen naturalist, who has spent a long life as gamekeeper and deerstalker in the Invergarry district, gives me in a letter the following interesting notes on what may be the last nesting of the osprey in Scotland. The nest was in a small fir tree on an islet of Loch Loyne, and was built by the end of April, 1910. By May 20 two eggs were laid. One of them was much smaller than the other and did not hatch. One young osprey was reared, and young and old disappeared that year at the end of July. The following spring (1911) one osprey returned to the nesting island in early May, but some mischance had evidently befallen the second bird, and after awaiting its mate in vain for some time the survivor left the district.

It is of course possible that a pair of ospreys have nested in the Scottish Highlands since that year, but if so it has not been recorded. Any bird lover would naturally keep an event of this kind to himself, and Murdoch Matheson informs me that he told no person at the time that the birds were hatching on Loch Loyne.

The summer of the year 1943 brought an unusual number of osprey records from different places in Scotland, and even England: I wonder whether the war then raging on the Finnish front may have disturbed the summer haunts of these birds and caused them to wander aimlessly; if so, there is a possibility that some old Highland nesting haunt may be repopulated. A friend of mine writes that he watched with pleasure that summer an osprey fishing on a well-known trout loch. The bird visited the loch in the forenoon and again in the late afternoon, flying across from a neighbouring wood.

One could wish that the osprey were as plentiful as another bird fisherman—the cormorant. The cormorant's voracity is proverbial, and it has few human friends. That it is disliked by birds also was shown me in a striking manner when I was fishing a loch in an Island glen one June day. Misty rain squalls drove across the loch and when the shower had passed sun and mist contended on the grassy slopes high above the water. Near the middle of the loch was a small island where a few pairs of common gulls were nesting. When first I arrived at the loch the gulls were restless and querulous, but gradually came to accept me as harmless and returned to their household duties. From a dark mist-cloud at the head of the glen a cormorant appeared, flying at speed down wind from the western ocean beyond the watershed. Above the loch it checked its flight and swung round into the wind in a wide circle, planing towards the water and evidently meaning to alight and fish there. This behaviour I viewed with apprehension, for on a small loch there is not room for a cormorant and a human angler. But I need not have worried. When the gulls saw the cormorant like a big black bomber descending heavily towards them they rose in a body and began to dive and dart at the great bird, uttering shrill and angry cries. Cormorants are birds of set purpose and I did not think that wanderer would be deterred by the unfriendly reception from alighting on and fishing in the loch: I was therefore surprised to see him hesitate, check his descent, then rise a little wearily into the air and continue his flight eastward toward the Firth of Lorne.

Where the small river leaves the loch a deep and still pool is formed, weedy and rush-grown. Salmon and sea trout run in from the sea and often rest in the pool before entering the loch. It is a hard pool to fish. The water is clear and there is no stream, so under ordinary conditions fine tackle would seem to be essential. But a salmon, or a moderate-sized sea trout, cannot be held here by fine tackle; he makes straight for the weeds or for the reeds—or for both—and is inevitably lost. There is nothing for it but to fish with one's strongest cast, and to achieve success it is necessary for the weather to be dark and stormy, preferably with a south-westerly gale which drives many small waves across the pool and prevents the fish seeing the cast, or the angler. But how seldom does the fisherman find conditions favourable here! He must trudge for miles across heather and bog, and when he arrives at the river the storm has passed, the sun is glinting on the pool, the air is calm, and, as though to mock him, silvery salmon and sea trout spring from the depths and at the end of their leap are poised for a moment like bars of burnished silver above the clear depths.

It was always a lonely glen, but there were two families here when I knew it first; now the old folk have passed, the houses are empty, and the glen is desolate and filled with the wild crying of curlew, wailing a coronach for the old days which will not return. But Glen More, Mull, is no stranger to tragedy nor to evil times. Here is Airidh na Sliseig, the Shieling of the Slicing or Beheading, commemorating the death by beheading of an old man and his three sons because of their refusal to yield up to their enemies the infant son (Murchadh Gearr) of MacLaine of Lochbuie. Here was decided the fight Blar Ceann a'Cnochain where Ewen of the Little Head fought with his followers against his own father MacLaine of Lochbuie, and was beheaded by the stroke of a claymore. The headless body remained in the saddle for almost a mile before it fell: an old cairn marks that tragic event. Here Donnchadh Donn, the Mull hunter lived; here, it is said, an enormous serpent once had his lair; here is the rock which on All Hallowe'en would foretell the future to those who enquired of it.

Now that tweed-making on the old hand-loom has almost died, the chief industry of the Hebrides are crofting and the fishing of lobsters off the rocky shores and around the surf-drenched islands.

The war has taken most of the younger men from the Islands, and the lobster fishermen are veterans, many of whom saw service in the war of 1914–1918. Lobsters were late in being controlled in price. It was fortunate for the lobster fishermen that the lobsters were controlled only at the end of the 1942–1943 winter, for the price until then, as I

A Crested Titmouse at home.

Kittiwake Gulls.

have elsewhere mentioned in this book, was high—up to 8/6 per lb. But even with the high prices then ruling the fishermen found it hard to make a living, for that winter was so wild that it was not possible to visit the creels set around out-lying islands for many days at a time and the numbers of creels swept away by the heavy seas made continued replacements necessary.

When Hebridean lobster fishermen are fishing round some remote island group they sometimes sleep for several nights in a roughly constructed bothy, or if there is no suitable harbour they may anchor the boat in the lee of the island and sleep in her. There is much labour in obtaining sufficient bait for the creels. Saithe (the young of the coal-fish) make excellent bait when they can be caught. Off the north-west coast of Skye is a small rocky island called Iasgeir. At the season of midsummer shoals of saithe swim around this island and are caught by the fly an hour or more after sunset. This means that the best fishing time is round about 1 a.m. by Midsummer Time and that the crew must be content with little sleep. As they row, with the bamboo rods over the stern of the boat, round the small isle rising in the track of the strong tidal rivers of the Minch, the fishermen hear the clamour of razorbill and guillemot, herring gull and kittiwake: they see the sun set in glory behind the dark cone of Clisham in Harris and watch the sunset glow creep from the north west through the north until it grows more bright on the north-east horizon, and the birth of another day has come.

Lobsters are kept in the sea in creels until there are a sufficient number to be sent away to the markets of the south. The crustacea must be packed with care, for a lobster arriving dead at the market is worthless. Even with the greatest care a consignment may sometimes arrive lifeless at Billingsgate: great heat is fatal to lobsters and frost is also deadly to them.

I mentioned Clisham, highest of Outer Hebridean hills. Here was the last haunt of the ptarmigan in the Outer Isles, but the race has now gone and the reason for its disappearance is so unusual that I must set it down here. There is little heather on Clisham and the slopes of the hill are covered with grass. The rabbits became very numerous on these slopes and ferrets were put down there. The ferrets preyed upon the rabbits, but they preyed upon the ptarmigan also, and, in my opinion, are undoubtedly responsible for the extermination of this bird. It is true that the eagle was blamed, but I think it unlikely that the eagle was the culprit, for the eagle has always had his home in that district and yet the ptarmigan had hitherto survived. It takes little to disturb the balance of nature. A friend of mine who owned an island on which he grazed cattle was perturbed by the increase of the island's rabbits, and set down a number of cats on the island to deal with those pests. It was unfortunate that the cats found the storm petrels more tasty than the rabbits and fed largely upon those small defenceless birds during their prolonged nesting period, which lasts from June to November. But now the cats in their turn have died and the storm petrels nest in peace.

There is still lamentable ignorance among the agricultural community about birds of prey. A circular was issued a short time ago by a Highland county agricultural organisation urging the farmers of that particular county to destroy all hawks, including the kestrel, at sight—and yet the kestrel is completely the farmer's friend, for its chief food is mice, and of late winters there has been, as I have mentioned in an earlier chapter, a plague of mice in the Western Highlands. The small rodents have destroyed corn stacks, made tunnels in the grass, eaten plants and bulbs in gardens, and have generally made themselves thoroughly objectionable. We could do with many more kestrels than we have, and this beautiful and graceful bird should be given full and strictly enforced protection. I was glad to read that the Secretary of State for Scotland had refused the county's petition to have the kestrel removed from the list of protected birds.

Ten years ago an aeroplane flying over a deer forest would have caused unrest, even panic among the deer over which it passed. But now deer, like most birds, have ceased to be alarmed. In 1943, on a summer day of blue sky and light, fleecy clouds, I flew from Orkney to Inverness. We passed close to the high cliffs of Hoy and to the Old Man of Hoy, a stack of Upper Old Red Sandstone 600 feet high, having at its base a zone of volcanic rocks which in turn rest upon the edges of tilted Lower Old Red Flagstones. Ahead of us, across the blue sun-lit water of the Pentland Firth, rose the cone of Morven, and when we had reached that hill, which is a part of the deer forest of Langwell, I could see a herd of red deer lying on the dry summit of a hill rather to the west of Morven. We passed low over the herd, yet the deer did not even trouble to rise nor to look up. In the same forest, ten years before, an aeroplane passing over the hill had moved every stag and spoiled the stalking for the day. When we were above Morven the whole range of the Cairngorms was visible over seventy miles away on the southern horizon, and it was possible to identify each hill, and the deep defile where the Lairig Ghru cuts through the range. As I travelled at speed above the hills I hoped that I might see a golden eagle sailing above this country of heather and bracken, bogs and lochs, and the pilot of the plane told me that a few days previously he had indeed passed an eagle ; he had recognised the bird by its great size and the up-turned primaries, widely spread.

Seeing the deer entirely unconcerned by the aircraft above them recalled to my mind a story I had heard a short time before. A lapwing had made her nest and laid her four eggs on the runway of an aerodrome, and at last she became so tame that she continued to brood her eggs while the heavy bombers passed over her, the pilots, who looked upon her almost as a mascot, being careful to handle their planes so that the tyres kept clear of her.

How high do red deer live in summer in Scotland ?. They rarely climb to the highest hill tops. I doubt if a stag has ever been seen on the top of Ben Nevis, 4,400 feet high and Britain's most lofty hill, nor do I ever remember seeing red deer on the summit of Ben MacDhui, 4,300 feet and highest of the Cairngorm range. In the finest summer weather deer are seen feeding on the green grass on Braeriach plateau, beside the Wells of Dee, 4,000 feet above sea level, but they are almost always hinds—as the female of the red deer is named. Hinds feed higher than stags in summer: I have known one drop her calf on Braeriach 3,600 feet above the sea. Deer sometimes climb high in summer in order that they may lie or play on the cool surface of some snowfield.

They are good weather prophets and if they are seen moving up (of their own free-will and not disturbed) to high ground it can be assumed that the weather is to be fine. When deer descend to low ground it is a sign of a break in the weather.

Ptarmigan, too, are sound weather prophets and I remember seeing them descending, on the wing and on foot, to a sheltered corrie before one of the worst winter blizzards I have experienced. It is well known that in the rutting season in October stags often roll in peaty holes to cool themselves but it is perhaps not so well known that they do this also in hot summer weather.

Many birds rear two broods of young in a season, but it is not often that the same nest is occupied. This happened on the Shin in the summer of 1943. A pair of dippers made their domed nest on a rock where anglers passed and repassed it only a few feet away. The first brood were successfully reared by May, and in early June the dippers laid a second clutch of eggs in the same nest, and were rearing their second family when I passed that way in the third week of the month.

I do not think that the Hebridean dipper, which has now, like the Hebridean thrush, been separated as a distinct species, usually rears two broods in the season; it may be that its food is not so plentiful here, or that the weather conditions are less favourable.

I have elsewhere in these pages written of the eagle which lays three eggs and usually rears three eaglets each year, and mentioned that although two pairs of eagles nested not far from each other on sheep ground no lamb has ever been taken. On that ground hares and rabbits are numerous, and I am sure that where its normal food supply is present the golden eagle very rarely carries off lambs. But there are districts where, owing to the wet, boggy nature of the hills, hares, rabbits and grouse scarcely exist. Here the eagle does at times turn its attention to lambs, and it would be surprising indeed were it otherwise. I was recently in a deer forest where, just over the 'march' a pair of eagles nest each spring. The stalker on the forest told me that in May the eagles took eight of his twenty-nine lambs, and fifteen or sixteen from a neighbouring sheep farm, but he had on only one occasion actually seen the eagle carrying a lamb to its eyrie. This reminded me that I was once told of a similar occurrence by a deerstalker who in the early summer was on the high ground. It was early in the day and there was thick mist in the glen but fine clear weather on the tops. An eagle came out of the mist. The bird had a lamb in its talons and passed so close to him that he could hear the lamb bleat.

But the harm an eagle does on sheep ground is infinitesimal compared to the damage wrought by a fox. I have elsewhere recorded the great increase in foxes during the years of war. On high ground, about 2,000 feet above sea level, on Foinne Bheinn in the Reay Forest, a fox's den was found in 1943. At this den were the head and legs of an oystercatcher. No oystercatcher nests anywhere near Foinne Bheinn: the bird may have been carried by the fox either from the north seacoast at Loch Eriboll, or from the western seaboard near Sandwood Bay. The distance from Loch Eriboll to Foinne Bheinn in a straight line is six miles, over very rough and boggy country. From Sandwood it is considerably further. It is possible (but not so likely, for the district is a populated one) that the oystercatcher was caught beside Loch Inchard, which is considerably nearer than Sandwood Bay, but, either from Loch Eriboll or from the Atlantic shore the climb to 2,000 feet must have been over rough, often boggy ground, and the first part of the journey over wet country, with many peat haggs and lochans in the way.

An instance of a black throated diver removing her eggs from one island to another has been reported to me by a deerstalker in northwest Sutherland. The original nesting place was a small grassy island

Berneray: in the Outer Hebrides.

Where the sea is the only road and man's back the only means of transport. Landing peats.

In the Reay Forest.

only a few feet in circumference. In mid-June after a heavy rainfall the loch rose until the island was awash. The diver was not seen to move her eggs, but two days after the spate was noticed sitting on another, rather larger, island about ninety yards distant. Here I saw the bird brooding, and visited the island at the end of the month, watching afterwards until the diver had returned and had climbed on to her nest. Their immersion must have rendered the eggs infertile; after a prolonged incubation of many weeks the bird abandoned them in late July.

There seems to be no doubt that this diver moved her eggs, because the pair was alone in the neighbourhood, and, as the stalker pointed out, it would have been impossible for the bird to have made a fresh nest and laid again in the course of two days.

This was in the same district where, the previous summer, I had watched a diver building up her nest to protect her eggs from a rising loch.

ith July has come the turn of the day. All too soon the long twilit nights are memories—precious memories —of the past. But there is a period for the first fortnight of the month when sunset and afterglow still merge with dawn on the red glowing horizon; when, from the north of Skye, the hills of Harris and Lewis stand at midnight black against that glory of light. It is as if the sweet spirit of midsummer is unwilling to leave land and sea which dream quietly in spiritual beauty. Because these hours are transient they are the more lovely, and are stored in the soul as a precious, indestructible memory.

The corncrake calls less frequently now, and the cuckoo is silent or almost so, but the Hebridean thrush still sings upon a wall or moss-crowned boulder, the corn bunting repeats his wheezy song, and the red throated diver fills the night air with strong barking cries, quickly repeated.

The fawns of the red deer are now growing fast and the mothers and their young may join into herds and climb to the high tops and corries where, during the heat of the day, they roll or lie on the snow-beds which are still found in July upon most of the lofty Scottish hills.

Hinds sometimes become pugnacious when they have young. One afternoon when an acquaintance and I were walking across a bracken-covered hill slope in the Isle of Mull a hind stood on the slope above us, eyeing us intently. We had heard that a hind on this hill had attacked a shepherd's dog and had put dog and shepherd to flight, and to see what would happen my companion set his collie dog at the hind. The long bracken hid the dog from the hind until he was near her but when she saw him a remarkable thing happened. Instead of running away she charged down the hillside at the approaching dog. The dog turned tail and made the best of his way down the hill, the hind only a few feet behind him. What would have been the end of it all I do not know, but my companion, fearing that the hind would strike and cripple his dog with her feet, shouted at the top of his voice. On hearing that angry human cry the hind desisted from her pursuit and walked away a short distance, still eyeing us malevolently from time to time.

On the same island a hind attacked a friend of mine—Mrs. Bryce Allan of Aros—while she was pulling sphagnum moss. As she was gathering the moss the animal without warning rushed at her from behind, hurling her headlong into some trees, fortunately with no worse injury than a bruised shoulder. Then the hind, stamping and showing her teeth, quickly advanced again to the attack, but hesitated when Mrs. Allan beat her on the nose with a thick stick which she was fortunately carrying at the time. A third time the hind attacked but was kept off by Mrs. Bryce Allan's dogs. It was decided to drive the plantation next day and kill the animal. The drive had scarcely started when the hind charged the gamekeeper, but was shot as she approached him. The animal had no calf, but a yearling of a good size was in the wood. Both these hinds lived comparatively near human habitations and frequently saw their inmates: perhaps the old adage is applicable to them, 'Familiarity breeds contempt.'

The great salmon rivers of Scotland which flow into the North Sea are at their best in spring or early summer, but on West Highland rivers July is the most productive month of the year. On the Dionard river, near the north-west seaboard of Sutherland, the best fishing month is July. I have had happy days fishing the Dionard with my friends Commander and Mrs. Fergusson. One midsummer day I recall when there had been a spate the evening before and the river was in grand order. For a month of fair weather you may fish the Dionard (you won't fish it at all in low water unless you are foolish) without a rise to reward you, for it is a river which is entirely dependent on rain. But if the rain comes at the right moment when fish are awaiting their opportunity to run up from the sea pools, grand sport is assured. Rain did come on this occasion, just at the right moment. There was a strong head of foaming amber-coloured water when I fished Heather Point that afternoon. I quickly landed a clean-run salmon of $7\frac{1}{2}$ lbs. at the head of the pool, and when about half way down, my fly a few minutes later was seized by a heavy fish. For half an hour I played him, and the longer I played him the more I was impressed by his size. I had strong gut and a stout rod, but do what I could I could not bring him to the shingle. After half an hour he was tiring and set off down stream; when he turned on his silvery side I saw that he was a very heavy fish, but shortly afterwards the fly came away and he remained resting, not on his side, but in a natural position in a 'stream' at the tail of the pool, near the bank and in perhaps two feet of water. I put on a monster fly, and tried to 'foul-hook' him with it. Time after time I scraped him with the fly, but the current was too swift for the hook to strike home. So played out was he that he took not the least notice of these attentions, which would have sent a fresh fish streaking like an arrow away to deep water. I then saw approaching Major A. Carmichael and his gillie John George MacKay, who had been fishing higher up the river. I walked over to them, told them what had happened, and asked them to come and see the fish, which had been lying in the same place for a good half hour. John George thought he might gaff the monster. Very cautiously he waded into the river, but as he poised himself for this critical action the salmon, sensing danger, swam slowly and sedately away into deep water.

In a letter to me in the autumn of the same year (1943) the Gualann keeper, George Ross, writes as follows:

'I saw the big fish in Heather Point several times during the season and she was twice hooked but broke the cast on each occasion. She was about 35 to 40 lbs. I saw her twice on the shallows above Heather Point during spawning. I am sure this is the fish Mr. Seton Gordon had a hold of in June.'

The fly with which I was endeavouring to 'foul-hook' the big fish was many sizes too big for fishing a river in summer temperature ('The lower the water temperature the bigger the fly' is a salmon-fishing maxim) but, to see what would happen, I went back to that part of the pool where I had hooked the great fish and made a cast. The fly had scarcely touched the water when a salmon almost as large as the fish I had lost sprang after it with a mighty splash. I was so greatly taken aback that I struck too soon, and so lost the opportunity of playing two exceptionally large fish on the same day in the same pool.

There seems to be little doubt that the salmon of the Dionard are considerably heavier than they were, or perhaps I should say there is a small proportion of much heavier fish than any caught in the river ten years ago. It has been suggested that the reason for this is to be found in the increase of weight in the salmon of a neighbouring river, the Laxford. Spawn brought from other rivers has produced a run of heavy Laxford salmon and I am told that in the streams in the neighbourhood heavy fish are now being seen.

The weather cleared shortly after I had lost my big fish, and the next day was cloudy, with little wind. Despite the reservoir of its loch the Dionard quickly falls, and the river was already on the low side, but good sport was expected provided the sun did not break through the thin covering of cloud which overspread the sky. Major Carmichael and I fished the upper water and as we passed the confluence of a burn with the parent stream a sandpiper left her eggs not a foot from the path. Under an overhanging bank at Heather Point a dipper was brooding her second clutch of white eggs with the music of the river in her ears. Alister Carmichael with John George MacKay left me to try Heather Point, and went farther up the river. They thought (and I agreed with them) that Heather Point was a certainty that morning and should yield several salmon. I started to fish the wine-coloured stream with high hopes and continued to cast with care and expectancy to the tail of the pool without rising a salmon or even seeing one move. This was discouraging, but I tried three more flies down the pool before I gave it up as a bad job. I then left to meet the others at Dugall's Run about a mile farther up the river. I walked fast, so as to waste as little as possible of the precious fishing time, for the river was falling rapidly. When I came in sight of Dugall's Run I saw that Alister Carmichael was playing a salmon, and when I reached him found that he had landed one fish and lost another. Salmon were moving freely in this 'run' and in Dugall's Pool below it, and it was not long before I rose and hooked a large fish, which was soon landed and weighed 24 lbs. I rose and lost another not much smaller—the salmon jumped right out of the water at the fly, and on these occasions one is apt to strike too soon, before the fly is properly in the salmon's mouth.

Dugall's Pool, very deep and black and with little current flowing through it, did not look a likely place for a fish that day but I saw a salmon show near the tail of the pool, where Dugall's Burn flows into it. When I put my fly over it the fish took it at once and I landed it—a salmon of 8 lbs. A little later Alister Carmichael played and landed a curious salmon. It had a large kelt-like head with the tooth-like projection from the lower jaw that is characteristic of the male kelt salmon. Yet at midsummer a kelt is an unheard-of thing, and this fish had sea lice on it, showing that it had come straight from the salt water, where no kelt would be found at that season. When we examined the fish we found that it had received a severe injury, perhaps from an otter or seal the previous season, and this had apparently prevented the salmon from regaining condition in the sea, so that it had remained in its 'kelt state' during its stay in salt water.

We finished our fishing when still four miles from home, and I do not think that John George MacKay is likely to forget that day, for he carried, making light of the weight, 73 lbs. of salmon back to the lodge, four miles distant and 500 feet above the river.

The next day was Sunday and no fishing is permissible in the Highlands on that day; public opinion would be gravely disquieted by it and besides it is illegal to fish on a Sunday for salmon in Scotland—but not in England. An anticyclone spreading over the Highlands brought then the finest of summer weather, and the Dionard shrank to a trickle, in which state it remained for weeks. Day after day the sky was cloudless, and for sixteen hours and more the sun shone with scorching heat, drying the bogs and the crofters' peats, waiting to be set up to harden.

One evening after supper my friend and Dara the collie—she who has been with me for many a walk through the glen, over the moor, and across the hill—left the Gualann to watch the sun set from Farraval, the hill on whose shoulder or *Gualann* the lodge is situated and from which it takes its name. We reached the broad top just before half past eleven at night (by the very artificial Double Summer Time, which is looked upon with little favour in the Highlands of Scotland). Although the sky at the zenith was clear a haze lay near the horizon, veiling from sight the long and low island of Lewis. Slowly the sun moved north above that distant horizon then, as it touched the sea, seemed spherical no longer but shaped like a lamp-shade, rich and warm from the kindly light within it. The lamp-shade later changed to a mushroom, the glowing stalk quenched in the sea. As the sun very slowly sank beneath the ocean perhaps seventy miles from us a pool of deep red was spilled upon that distant sea. At eighteen minutes to twelve he was gone, to light that Celtic land of the spirit, Tir nan Og, and Foinne Bheinn then lost her purple glow and her cone-shaped summit became grey and cold. Like a jewel, Loch Dionard lay amethystine at the head of its glen. A golden plover rose and flew swiftly over Farraval. The sea breeze went to rest, its dying airs leaving scattered pathways upon the ocean's face.

It is said that God gave us Memory, that we might have roses in December: I like to remember this, and other sunsets, during the short days, the dark days of winter, and the dark days of life.

That evening we did not see the eagles that often soar above Farraval, hunting the hares that live on the higher slopes of the hill.

A correspondent has written to ask me how it is that the eagle has the unique gift of renewing its youth; he recalls the verse in the Psalms, Ps. CIII, v. 5, and wonders if I am able to explain it. When first I received the letter I could think of no scientific ground for this belief, nor of any tradition to support it, but then I recalled that in the Isle of Lewis there is a tradition bearing on the matter.

This tradition came to my knowledge in rather a curious way. I had given a nature talk on the eagle and other birds at one of the island schools, and some weeks afterwards the headmaster sent me a number of the essays which the scholars had written on my talk. When I read the essays I was interested that several of the writers mentioned a thing I had never told them of—that the eagle does indeed renew its youth. The story was as follows: When the eagle reaches old age the curve of its beak becomes so pronounced that it is no longer able to tear the carcase of its prey. The eagle, feeding with difficulty, becomes old and feeble, then one day its instinct, or its wisdom, causes it to mount high into the air and, swooping earthward, to strike its bill against a rock or stone. By this impact the point of the bill is broken and the bird is now able to feed with ease. Thus, in the words of the Psalmist, its youth is renewed. When I wrote to the schoolmaster about this and asked him what had made the scholars describe an incident which I had not mentioned, he said that the tradition was firmly held in at least two parishes of Lewis—Barvas and Uig. He told me that he had recently heard the same story from a man in the village of Borve. This man was at the time (1932) in his seventieth year, and remembered hearing the tradition from a very old man in the same village who died more than fifty years before. A slight variant in the story came from the lips of the schoolmaster's own father, an old man of ninety at the time. According to him the eagle did not fly into the air and then dash its bill on a stone, but merely stood upon a rock and struck and rubbed the bill upon it until the curving projection of the upper mandible broke away.

The Celts came originally from the east, and it is an interesting thought that the tradition which the Psalmist had in mind when he wrote his immortal verse may have been the same that is recalled by the peat fire in the Isle of Lewis at the present day.

A curious incident was reported to me from the hill country between Crieff and Comrie, in the county of Perth. I will tell the story in my correspondent's own words:

'My eldest boy, aged eleven, was fishing a burn, a quarter of a mile from my cottage on the moor. He had caught a brown trout of a quarter of a pound, laid the fish on the bank, and begun to bait his hook with a fresh worm a few feet away. Suddenly there was a rush of wind and a large bird "the size at least of a capercaillie," as my boy said, descended on his trout and carried it off in its talons. My son was so alarmed that he ran home. He is definite that the bird carried off the fish in its *claws* and was dark in colour, the neck being red or russet. I have since taken him to the Edinburgh Zoo, where he saw a golden eagle and a buzzard. He considers that the eagle is most like the bird that stole his best trout of the day. A pair of eagles did indeed nest that year only a few miles from the scene of the incident, but as a trout is unlikely fare for the eagle I thought I might refer the matter to you.'

My first thought on reading the letter was that the bird must have been an osprey, but the great size and the red on the neck are against this theory: the osprey besides does not now nest in Scotland and is found in our country only as a rare passage migrant. Whether the bird was eagle or osprey, it showed remarkable dash and bravery in swooping down and taking the trout from the angler's feet.

Eagles capture strange prey at times. I have seen several squirrels in an eyrie and more than one stoat. A shepherd in the Inner Hebrides was on the hill one day when an eagle rose near him. He went to the spot, and there found the bird's 'kill'—a ferret. Some years before a number of ferrets had been liberated about twenty miles away from the scene of the occurrence, to keep down the rabbits, and had spread widely over the surrounding district.

A ferret is a formidable animal for even the eagle to kill; perhaps this one was asleep in the sun and was taken unawares. When it was disturbed the bird had not begun to feed, but had partly skinned the ferret and had torn some of its fur off.

The golden eagle is uncommon, but not rare in the Scottish Highlands: the white-tailed or sea eagle, sometimes called the erne, is now extinct as a breeding species, although migrants from time to time are reported, not only from Scotland but from England also. In March 1932 it was reported in the press that an eagle—in all probability a wandering sea eagle—had been shot at Whitfield, in the county of Dover. This is a bird protected by Act of Parliament, and as I saw no further report in the press that the man who shot the bird had been prosecuted, I wrote to Ramsay MacDonald, the Prime Minister, on the matter, only to learn, through the Attorney-General, that the case had been dismissed on the plaintiff paying the sum of 4/- costs. To bird-lovers a penalty of 4/- for shooting a rare bird is inadequate, to say the least.

Some people who carry a gun cannot resist slaying anything beautiful or unusual. How blind and incomprehending are these so-called sportsmen. Were they to observe and venerate, their knowledge would be the richer—and not only would they themselves benefit, but others would be able to enjoy the same beauty. The war had loosed a flood of hate and misunderstanding, yet I do not think that in the future nature lovers will be fewer, but rather that they will increase and make their voices more and more heard. It may be said that the eagle does harm on grouse moors by killing and frightening the grouse, but a friend of mine, a great nature lover, shot 544 brace of grouse on a Sutherland moor on which nested that year one pair of golden eagles, one pair of peregrine falcons, five pairs of ravens, two pairs of merlins, and eight pairs of kestrels. In addition to these birds, which are usually classed as vermin, many wild cats and several pairs of pine martens had their home on the ground.

The sight of the golden eagle is extraordinarily keen. A correspondent who stalked chamoix in the Tyrol gives me an interesting example of this. He had killed and gralloched a chamois and had left the entrails on a rock, on which there was also a pool of blood from the slain animal. An eagle more than a mile distant saw the blood and the entrails and at once approached and alighted at the rock. My correspondent had no doubt that it was sight, not smell, which had enabled it to track its food.

There are traditions in the Highlands—they are all old traditions now—that eagles have on occasion taken children to their eyries. These traditions I think refer to the white-tailed eagle, for it was a larger and more powerful bird than the golden eagle. Mr. Hugh Douglas, who was factor on the MacDonald estate in the Isle of Skye a good many years ago, informs me that about the year 1900 the late Miss Flora MacKinnon of Duisdale told him that as a young girl she had seen an old, large man, known as Niall Iolair, Neil Eagle. He had received this name because, as a baby, he had been the hero of a strange adventure. One day of summer when the people of Raasay had gone to the hill to cut or stack their peats, Neil, with other very young children, had been carried up to the hill with their parents. It was the custom to do this, and to tether each child firmly by the leg, to prevent its wandering. For some reason Neil's mother had left her little son free, and a passing eagle swooped down and carried the child over the sea channel to Skye. Here, at Skeabost, the eagle alighted with the boy. It happened that people working in the fields near saw the bird with its strange burden, ran to the place, and found the infant unhurt.

The Highland crofter is busy, these July days. The peats must be carted home from the hill and stacked, and whenever the sun shines (which is seldom) the hay must be cut with the scythe and 'cured' as they call it in the west. I often think of the climate of the Hebrides and compare it with the weather of more favoured lands. What would be the reaction of the Hebridean crofter to the climate of Italy? He has been called sad and gloomy, mournful and lethargic. Were he to live beneath clear sunlit skies his character would be very different. His work is one continual struggle against adversity. The hay is perhaps cut and spread, the evening is fine and clear, and all preparations are made to put up the hay next day. But towards midnight an ominous haze appears on the southern horizon, the wind rises, rain begins to fall. In the morning wind and rain hold revelry; the hay is wet and sodden; there is nothing to be done but to wait, perhaps for many days, for the next dry spell of weather. From the south west blows the sea wind, day after day in July. It brings always wet weather to the west, but along the eastern seaboard of Scotland fine, dry weather is experienced with the south-west wind.

The rate of pay for labourers in the Hebrides, as elsewhere, compares favourably with the remuneration of olden times. I was in conversation recently with a man whose great-great-grandfather assisted at the building of the Manse of Kilmuir in Skye 200 years ago. My informant said that all the sand used in the building operations was carried over the moor from the stream at Lacasaidh, a good mile distant. The way was arduous and boggy; the pay sixpence for a day's work!

In Hebridean fields the corn bunting broods her eggs or feeds her young in July, sometimes paying the penalty of late nesting by having her nest laid bare by the scythe. Even if the eggs be seen in time and a small area of long grass left round them, the birds usually desert. A few of the crofters own horse-drawn reapers, and these may decapitate young corncrakes, or even the parent birds. The corncrake, as I have recorded elsewhere in this book, is everywhere decreasing, for it finds modern methods of swift reaping little to its liking. A horse-drawn reaper is bad enough, but when it is swiftly propelled by a motor the nestlings are relentlessly pursued and cut to pieces. The time will come when the corncrake will be as rare as the osprey or the sea eagle. Last July our man, scything a field of rye grass, unfortunately killed two baby corncrakes with his scythe. They were already at the stage when they could walk or run with ease and it might have been thought that the parents would have moved the rest of the brood, but next day the scythe killed a third almost in the same place. The previous year in August our reaper had decapitated three young corncrakes.

One July day I was walking along an old track at the fringe of the cultivated area on the north-west wing of Skye. The day was fine and sunny and a sea breeze was blowing, its strength perhaps twelve miles an hour. Above a grassy slope I saw a small bird suspended motionless, kestrel-like, and when I approached I saw that it was a wheatear. Using its tail to balance it, and with wings rapidly driven, the bird kept its station, watching intently for any insect moving in the grass below. Then there was a quick stoop, the prey was caught and eaten, and the bird rose aloft once more, to hang suspended in the same fashion. I could see that the tail was depressed and continually moving, and one wing was sometimes held pendulous, as an additional aid to its balance. This little bird was hovering more delicately and skilfully than any kestrel, and it was strange to see it thus, for I had not heard of, nor seen, a wheatear hovering in this way before.

Although the kittiwakes have become scarcer, these war years, the razorbills keep up their numbers. There is one small colony on the basaltic face of Tuilm Island, off the north-west coast of Skye, which always gives me pleasure. The dark rock is worn, perhaps by the action of waves in bygone ages, into small hollows or 'pockets' and these the razorbills use. One bird fits well into each 'pocket', and of a July evening when the sun shines and the wind has died they may be seen peering out over the green sea and perhaps panting with the heat. They are late in laying the single handsome egg and this is not hatched until mid-July. The young razorbill may be seen looking out from the shelter of its parent's feathers, watching the herring gulls that wheel and dive and call with high, strident voices, but it is not long before the chick is shepherded out to sea by one of the parents, there to lead an oceanic life until in its turn it comes to land to rear its young. It is worth placing on record that never have I seen both parents at sea with the young razorbill. It is the same with the guillemot, and it may be that the second parent is away fishing and returns only to feed the young.

It is curious that swallows and house martins should on occasion search for a nesting site late in the summer. Last July (1943) a pair of swallows appeared early in the month and began to fly in and out of our motor shed. The nearest pair of nesting swallows are at Uig, six miles from where we live, and these may have been young birds from a brood of the previous season. We hoped that they might remain to nest with us, but there was no hole by which they could enter and leave except when the door of the shed was open, and after a few days they departed. In the previous chapter I have mentioned the late nesting of house martins in Aberdeenshire.

The lapwing or green plover would seem to be extending its range in the Highlands. A few years ago I found it nesting on the western Cairngorms at a height of almost 3,000 feet above the sea where previously it was unknown. That was a decided extension of its range into the hill country. It is also extending its seaward range: in July 1943 I found that it had taken up its nesting quarters on Fladday Chuain, a small flat isle lying far out in the Minch between Skye and Harris. On this isle hundreds of barnacle geese have their winter home and in summer a colony of Arctic terns sometimes nest here, but it was unexpected to find a pair of nesting lapwing on my visit. They had young at the time and if they succeeded in rearing their brood a new colony may in time be founded here. When ocean birds are decreasing at their Hebridean haunts, and corncrake and corn bunting are becoming scarcer on land, it is pleasant to think that at least one species is on the increase.

In most places lapwings are seen in flocks in their winter quarters, but with us in Skye they appear more often singly—a lonely spirit rising suddenly from the storm-vexed earth and flying as though in mute protest unsteadily into the winter twilight.

A friend of mine was stationed for a time on Salisbury Plain during the war. She was impressed by the number of birds on that wind-swept plain and of the lapwings she wrote that they 'toss themselves against the clouds with lonely cries'. I like that brief, poetic description, which brings so clearly to the mind the rising of lapwing into the air during a day of wind.

Earlier in this chapter I recorded the skilled kestrel-like hovering of a wheatear on the watch for insects above a hill slope. Another incident in which a wheatear figured I recall. It was on the Cairngorms, and I had climbed from Glen Feshie early in the morning. At a height of 3,000 feet the sun shone dim through the fog and then, more quickly than it takes to tell, I had walked out of that sea of mist and saw all the hill country ahead of me glorious in the light of the unclouded sun. As I looked back I could see the mist gently eddying in the corrie below me, and as I watched that scene of beauty a wheatear, rising from stony ground, flew delicately into the air and with soft inconsequent song saluted the mastery of the sun over the clouds.

I had hoped that day to see the cushion pink still in flower on the stony plateau of Braeriach, 4,000 feet above the sea, but even at this height its season of flowering was over, and I had begun to think that I should not see, nor smell the perfume of one of the most delightful flowers of the high tops when, at the edge of the great corrie which separates Braeriach from Cairntoul, I came upon many plants in blossom. The snow had not long melted here—indeed the remains of a drift, discoloured by debris, still remained—and thus the flowering season of the plants had been retarded. It was pleasant to sit awhile at the edge of the corrie, the heat of the sun tempered by a cold breeze blowing off the perpetual snowbed at the head of the Garbh Choire about 400 feet below, for the honey-scent of *silene* flowers was in that breeze and although the plateau elsewhere was parched the ground here was still damp from the lately melted snow. That day I saw no mountain hares at this elevation but some years before I found, almost on the 4,000 feet contour line, a 'form' of perhaps the highest-born leverets in Scotland. Not far from where the Wells of Dee spring ice-cold from the depths of the earth, in a tussock of dry grass I came upon, one June day, several young leverets in their nest. There was little shelter for them at this great height, seven hundred feet above the heather line and even above the nesting ground of the ptarmigan. Of the parent hares I saw no sign; they did not perhaps wish to advertise their presence on that bare plateau.

But to return to the day on which, beneath the strong sun, I sat high above the snows that remain unmelted from one year to another and saw the pink flowerets and rosy buds of *silene acaulis*. The biting deer fly or cleg, one of the family of Tabanidae, was high that day, and I was bitten by one of these insects on the shoulder of Cairntoul at a height of 3,750 feet above sea level—at a greater elevation than I have ever seen one of these pests before. It had no doubt followed up the stags which, later that day, I watched at the edge of a peat hagg. The flies were causing the deer considerable discomfort and their long, flexible ears were continually being moved, so that for a time they hung for a brief second pendulous. They rolled in the wet peat; they shook themselves like dogs, and when at last I had no more leisure to watch them but had perforce to show myself and continue my journey toward the east, the startled herd gathered together and made off at their best speed.

Some days on the hill are of unusual interest. As I was walking through Glen Giusachan of Mar, fragrant with bog asphodel and bell heather, I saw a reddish object in the fresh green ling ahead of me. As I approached, an intervening ridge hid the object for a time, and when next I was in sight of it I saw that it was a fox. Reynard was now only a few yards from me but so intent was she (for I was near enough to see that it was a vixen) on a scent she was following through the heather that she had no idea danger was near. Nose to the ground, she moved with a gliding motion a few yards, then stopped to rest. Sometimes she half-closed her eyes and panted slightly, for the sun was warm. Her thick brush was very light in colour, so that it seemed almost white against the heather. Several meadow pipits hovered in an agitated manner above her, and she may have been searching for their nests and young. For a considerable time I watched her, and had it not been that a long journey still lay ahead of me I might have learnt some of her secrets; but at length it was necessary for me to show myself and at once she made all speed up the glen, pausing only for a brief second to glance back, as though she found it hard to believe she had permitted a man to approach so near to her. It may have been only a coincidence that I saw not a single grouse that day during a ten-mile walk through a land where I might have expected to have seen at least a dozen pairs of these birds, with or without their young.

It is ironical that the pleasure of the finest August days in the Highlands—and especially in the Western Highlands and the Hebrides—should be impaired, or even entirely spoilt, by the onsets of the midge.[1] This pest loves heathery lands, but attacks the climber even on the bare rocky tops of the Cuillin, three thousand three hundred feet above the Atlantic. The midge prefers damp, calm weather, but is active even during cloudless August days, awaiting the lessening of the sun's power and appearing in myriads in the late afternoon, to feast upon any luckless wanderer in its path. I recall the opening days of a recent August before the outbreak of the World War when the shade temperature in Glen Sligachan beneath the Cuillin was in the eighties and the sun shone with tropical heat. The family and I were in Glen Sligachan that day, in Harta Corrie where the huge boulder, Clach a' Phuill, the Stone of Blood, commemorates a clan fight between the MacDonalds and the MacLeods. During the homeward walk in the early evening the sun was still high, and, since the air was very still and we made our own wind current as we walked, no midge was felt. When we reached the road at Sligachan, where we had left the car, I was some distance behind the others. We were all weary after a long day on the hill, and were looking forward to our tea, which we had left in the open car. When I came in sight of the car I saw that the family, instead of sitting comfortably in it and enjoying this well-earned tea, were walking briskly up and down the road. At first I was at a loss to understand the reason for this apparent unnecessary haste and exertion; then the ominous word, 'Midges', flashed across my mind. When I reached the car things were even worse than I had imagined. It may be that the human scent pervading a car attracts the midge as carrion does a fox. Whatever be the reason it is certain that a stationary car *does* attract them. On this occasion the car was literally veiled in a thin mist—myriads upon myriads of midges dancing above the windscreen and hood, swarming upon bonnet and wings. I had time only to snatch a cup of tea and a scone before being set upon, and was then glad to do my four miles an hour on the hard road while I quickly finished that afternoon meal.

In Sutherland I have known road reconstruction actually put a stop to by the attacks of midges. Some anglers in that midge-infested county wear special veils when fishing, and certain gardeners in the Isle of Skye are provided with these veils by their employers.

[1] Midges make their appearance early in some parts of the West Highlands. On May 30, 1944, they were very active at Craignure, Mull, in bright sunshine, though they had not then appeared in the north of Skye.

It is late in August before the twilight which has persisted throughout the night in June and July is replaced by darkness. It is then that the first display of the aurora or Northern Lights is seen. The Celt named these mysterious lights Na Fir Chlis, The Nimble Men, and nimble they are, and incredible is the speed at which they travel from northern horizon to zenith. The usual colour of the aurora is white, with a pale greenish tinge; very rarely a blood-red display is seen. Readers of this chapter may remember the remarkable display of red aurora that was visible on the last day of January, 1940. The aurora is normally a northern phenomenon: it is seen frequently in Scotland, more rarely in England, and very seldom indeed south of that country. But this great display was seen in Spain and Portugal and even in Africa, and so red was the sky that many people thought that the glow of some vast and distant fire was reflected in the heavens. There is an old tradition that a display of red aurora is seen only before some great disaster: that display, at all events, came when mankind was at the beginning of a very dark avenue. My most vivid impression of this strange auroral display was the deepness—the blood-like quality—of the great pools of red which appeared at the zenith, waxing and waning slightly, changing their position, and dimming the light of the stars. From west to east that night a broad ray of light, very bright and clear, spanned the heavens. It was like an immense searchlight and was very faintly tinged with red. It was entirely distinct from the lesser greenish rays that were rising from the northern horizon and from the pools of red that, nearer the zenith, lay bodingly in the black velvet dome of the sky.

The aurora assumes many forms, the most usual being a glowing arc on the northern horizon, from which shoot up green-tinted rays that wax and wane. There are, too, great pulses of light that move at incredible speed from horizon to zenith; the only thing which I have seen that reminded me of them were small pools of moonlight late one October evening at the crest of Lairig Ghru, that hill pass of the Cairngorms. The moon, near the full, was invisible, but at times the racing clouds thinned, and then a pool of warm orange light raced across the dark slopes of Braeriach, crossed the Lairig, and sped away up the rocks of Creag an Leth-choin beyond it.

On the mainland the early part of August is often a time of thunderstorms. In the Hebrides there are few thunderstorms in summer. One of these I watched from my study window late at night, as dusk was creeping over the sea. At ten o'clock a very dark, compact cloud formed far across the Minch, over the Outer Hebridean isle of North Uist or beyond it. At intervals that black, brooding cloud was

Looking across to Cairntoul from Monadh Mór.
A refreshing drink from an icy spring.

Red Deer in the Forest of Mar. Carn a' Mhaim and Monadh Mór in
the background.

Dara in the Reay Forest, with the knife-like ridge of Foinne Bheinn, five miles long, in the background

suffused with the glow of still more distant lightning, or a dart of lightning pierced it to the sea below. That momentary flash of gold through the cloud was very lovely and rare to see against the ebbing sunset.

Summer thunderstorms in the Hebrides are often followed by fog which creeps in from the sea in grey clouds, damp, clammy and cold. Mist is the seaman's enemy: he must grope his way blindly through it. One day I looked out over the Minch, above which a low fog hung. I saw there a strange thing—the tops of the masts of a passing steamer and a feather of brown smoke from an invisible funnel rising into the clear air. Those responsible for the navigation of that craft must have been having an anxious time, for the Minch here is bestrewn with rocky islands and the navigation channel is not wide. They could not tell that at the fore mast-head there was clear weather. In the same manner we grope often in material mist when spiritual beauty is just above us, beyond the view of our fog-ridden senses.

On a dark, thundery day I was traversing the Cairngorms, the air heather-perfumed on the lower slopes. At the Pools of Dee I reached a favourite haunt of the ptarmigan and first one, then several of these white-winged birds, rose snorting from the grey rocks. The ptarmigan I had expected to see; the small flight of teal which rose from one of the Pools and winged their way fast southward were unexpected. I had never before seen any bird save a dipper on the Pools of Dee. They lie nearly 3,000 feet above sea level, and there is no vegetation growing in their ice-cold waters. The teal (it was late August) were probably on migration, like the swallows which I saw shortly after sunrise one morning in late summer here. I had walked across from Aviemore to Braemar to assist in the judging of the piping at the Braemar Gathering and as I was expected to do the same thing at the Kingussie Gathering the next day it was necessary for me to return through the Lairig Ghru very early the next morning in order to reach Kingussie in time. It was a perfect morning. I saw the sun rise on Braeriach and Cairntoul and shortly after its rising reached the Pools of Dee. There, in the faery light of that glowing sun, I wondered for an instant if my eyes were not playing me a trick, for I saw what at first glance appeared to be small animals travelling snakelike at tremendous speed along the rock-strewn pass. Then I realised that these were no terrestrial creatures but a flight of swallows, winging their way toward the south a foot or more off the ground. So low did they fly that I could look down on them and admire the lovely dark-blue plumage of their backs. Like the teal, they were on migration and had perhaps passed the night somewhere along the valley of the Spey and before sunrise had set off on their journey through the hills. How different was the weather that early morning in late summer to the conditions which had forced down the robin that in spring I had found lying lifeless on deep snow here!

In our garden in Skye a solitary young robin usually appears in early August. He is then a brown, inconspicuous bird, but soon begins to assume his red breast. When anyone appears in the garden the robin flies up to them, hoping that the human friend will, by weeding or digging, expose an earthworm or other titbit. His appetite is voracious, and when his wants are for the moment satisfied he flies off to some bush, and in a few minutes is back again, hungry as ever. His dexterity in swallowing an earthworm is remarkable: he holds it crosswise in his bill, and in the twinkling of an eye it has disappeared down his throat. Robins do not nest in the immediate vicinity although they may rear their young on boulder-strewn ground, where a few stunted birches battle against the storms, a few miles from us. A winter or two ago we had an equally tame robin, which was one day missed and was presumed to have fallen a victim to a hawk or cat. But some time afterwards its mummified body was found in a disused room, into which, unknown to is, it must have flown for food or shelter. In frosty weather this robin used to come with me to the peat stack and while I loaded the peats into a barrow kept a keen watch for any insects, flying down fearlessly to my feet or perching on the barrow to pick them up. Even a large and formidable centipede travelling at speed was seized by the robin and swallowed with ease: it seemed indeed to have less difficulty with a centipede than with a worm. The Rev. Murdo MacLeod, minister of Kilmuir in Skye, had a robin in his motor shed one winter. He used to feed the bird and told me that so far as he knew, it never went outside, thus showing commonsense, for the winter was a wet and stormy one. That robin knew no English; my friend conversed always with it in Gaelic, which is still the language of Skye.

In *Edward Grey and his Birds* I have recorded the fearlessness of the robins which Viscount Grey tamed at Fallodon. One of the photographs in that book shows a robin in full song perched on Lord Grey's hat. Many robins fed from Edward Grey's hand, but until the last spring of his life none of them had flown on to his head after being fed, there to sing a short song of thanks—this I think was one of the triumphs in the life of a great statesman and a man of singular charm and uprightness.

One August day I was the witness of a rather curious incident in the lives of a pair of ravens which nest in the neighbourhood and are frequently seen flying, either singly or together, over our house. There was a stiff north-easter blowing at the time, the aftermath of a thunderstorm, and the ravens were making their way with their characteristic powerful flight into the teeth of the wind. I was on the top of a grassy, rock-strewn hill and the ravens were passing rather below me: although they were near they did not observe me as I sat on the grass. One of the ravens suddenly swung round, hovered kestrel-like (I have never seen a raven hover before), soared for a few seconds on the breeze, then swooped down and quite near me took what seemed to be a mouse or shrew from the steep hillside. The raven then flew across to a knoll, quickly tore up and swallowed the prey, and then seeming to say to itself 'By Jove, I must hurry after my mate' made the best speed possible in the direction the second bird had taken. I have noticed that when a raven, flying with its mate, checks its flight to investigate possible food, the mate continues on its course, and I have wondered how the two find one another again—probably by sight, which in the raven is very keen.

A raven rarely if ever attacks a dog, but a shepherd recently told me that when he was on the hill an eagle swooped at his collie, diving down upon the dog 'with a scream'. The dog sprang into the air at the eagle, which then flew away.

After its first flight from the eyrie the young eagle is rarely seen in the neighbourhood of the nesting site. One August afternoon as I was walking along the edge of a cliff where a pair of eagles nest I noticed the young eagle perched on a pinnacle ahead of me: when it flew I could see plainly the area of white feathers on the tail which distinguishes the young golden eagle from the adult, and sometimes results in its being confused by observers with the very rare white-tailed eagle. When the young eagle had mounted a little way into the air it was joined by its parents. It returned to the rock and later took a much longer flight, being accompanied by one of the old birds to a considerable height above the ground. I watched through my glass the youngster fly perhaps a mile from the rock, then from a good height return in a masterly slant, with wings motionless and held back half-closed, to its perching place on the cliff.

Eagles are silent birds, but a Highland gamekeeper told me that he was on the hills one day when he heard what he thought was the barking of a terrier coming from a high rock near. Thinking that a dog might have fallen over the cliff, or that it might have found a fox's earth, he hurried to the place. He then saw that a pair of eagles were sailing across the face of the cliff in play, swooping and diving at each other and all the time uttering strong barking cries which in the still hill air had carried a long distance.

In early May whimbrel, on their northward flight to Iceland, visit the Hebrides in small flocks, very tame and friendly, and in this respect differing from their larger relatives the curlew. Late in August they visit us again, but this time singly and almost furtively, haunting the seaweed-covered shore at low tide and not the green machair as in spring. White wagtails also visit us in August on their way south from Iceland to their winter quarters. The white wagtail is a paler and less boldly marked bird than its relative the pied wagtail. One of them I watched outside the house on a gusty August day. So fierce were some of the gusts that they caught the dainty little bird and swung it round in an almost complete circle, but it remained unperturbed under those buffetings and continued, when the wind permitted it do do so, to chase the insects on which it fed. Is there, I wonder, any special virtue in the wagtail tribe's long tail? In strong and gusty winds it is certainly a handicap to the bird.

A curious nesting site was once chosen by a pair of pied wagtails. A bird-loving friend of mine, Major W. H. Hunt, who was engineering the new road through Glencoe to the south some years ago, has given me the details of that strange nesting place. The scene was the main quarry from which the road metalling and stone for the bridges was obtained, near the county boundary between Perth and Argyll, 1,000 feet above sea level. In this qarry was a pandemonium of noise— the gun-like hammering of the drills, periodic earth-shaking detonations when the rock was blasted, a stone-crusher constantly at work, and trolleys being run frequently backwards and forwards over the small railway tracks, produced a deafening and jarring chorus. Despite this the wagtails decided upon that quarry as their nesting place and unfortunately chose a part where the rock had to be blasted before the eggs hatched. Shortly before the detonation charge was fired in the rock the workmen carefully lifted the nest from its place in the quarry-side, set it down in the centre of the quarry, and built around it a small splinter-proof shelter between two of the railway tracks. The wagtails found the nest in its new site—or they may have watched it being placed there—survived that blasting and many others, hatched their eggs and reared their brood. From the foreman downward all the men in the quarry regarded those wagtails with the most tender affection. They were rough men, some of them had more than once been up against the law and had got the worst of it, yet those dainty and confiding birds appealed to the better side of their nature, and had anyone interfered with either eggs or young it would have gone hard indeed with him.

The same friend had on one occasion unusual opportunities for watching the family life of a pair of rabbits.

Early in the summer two tons of sand were dumped at the side of a fence, six yards from his window. Shortly after midsummer, at eleven o'clock one night, my friend saw a rabbit near and noticed that a small hole had been dug in the sand. Next morning the hole was closed. When a week had gone by and nothing further had apparently happened my friend's wife (unknown to him) very carefully made three side shafts to intercept the burrow, and when she slowly inserted her hand received the surprise of her life when she felt her fingers softly nibbled! The entrances to the side shafts were now carefully closed and smoothed out, and that night the two nature lovers watched to see what would happen.

About ten o'clock (this was by Double Summer Time) the two old rabbits arrived and began to feed on some short grass near, but appeared entirely to ignore the heap of sand. About 11 p.m. the male approached, mounted the sand heap, and sniffed suspiciously around where human hands had worked. The rabbit then disappeared and at midnight the observers, seeing nothing further, went to bed.

My friend slept uneasily that night and at 4 a.m. awakened and looked out of the window. He was rewarded by seeing the female rabbit (the doe) slowly opening the burrow. She was excavating a very little of the sand at a time, then pausing to look up and see whether she was observed. The buck rabbit was watching near, and occasionally gave a warning by stamping quickly on the ground with his hind pads, at the same time flicking up his tail and showing the white. At each warning his mate quickly left the burrow. Two strange rabbits, much smaller and younger than the pair with the burrow, were the cause of these warnings. While the owners of the nest were chasing away the larger of the two intruders the smaller of that pair had the temerity to run up and sniff the entrance to the burrow. This impudence made Mother Rabbit particularly angry, and she was not content until both the unwelcome visitors had been driven well away. She then returned to the burrow and slowly and carefully continued her excavations. When at last she had cleared the entrance she crouched in front of it with her head out (carefully watching the while) and my friend then noticed that she was suckling her young ones, which received only one meal during the twenty-four hours.

When the family had been fed she filled in the hole by backing down it, then scooping the sand towards and under her. When she could scrape in no more sand in this way she wriggled out of the hole, turned round, and scooped in as much sand as was necessary to finish the job of blocking the entrance. She then smoothed and beat down the sand with her nose, but was careful to leave a small air hole about one inch in diameter at the top of the filling. My friend said that although he subsequently watched her several times while she was filling in the burrow he could never discover how she was able to leave open this air shaft, which was vital for the young, to enable them to breathe.

The hole was usually closed by 5.30 or 6 a.m.—that is by 3.30 or 4 a.m. G.M.T.

In the Highlands August is the seatrout month *par excellence* for, unlike salmon, seatrout rarely run into fresh water in early spring or indeed until mid-summer. A very heavy seatrout was killed on a Dunkeld fly (size No. 12) in August, 1943, in Loch Stack in Sutherland. The fish weighed $18\frac{1}{2}$ lbs. and was the heaviest recorded from Loch Stack; perhaps indeed the heaviest seatrout taken in Scotland with rod and fly. The girth of this great fish was $19\frac{1}{4}$ inches, the length 33 inches, the tail 9 inches and the small of the tail $7\frac{3}{4}$ inches. It was believed to have spawned twelve times and to have been about twenty years old. I am told that in 1908 a seatrout of $19\frac{1}{2}$ lbs. was taken on the Tay, but this fish I understand was caught by the nets in the tidal waters.

The grey or hooded crow is greatly on the increase in the Western Highlands and Islands at the present time. This large grey-backed crow, a powerful bird with a slovenly flight, is a crafty fellow, and his misdeeds are many. He is an omniverous feeder, and devours the eggs and young of any bird not powerful enough to defend itself and its brood. He attacks full-grown larks and more than once I have seen a grey crow in hot and relentless pursuit of an unfortunate lark, which was very weary when I came on the scene and whose life I think I may have saved—for the time being at all events—by driving off the crow. The grey crow is almost unique among birds in that he can count. It is therefore useless for the bird photographer to take only one companion with him to his hide. Other birds are satisfied when they see that one person leaves the hide after two people have arrived at it, and do not realise that one of the two has remained in concealment. Not so the hooded crow. This my wife and I proved conclusively when attempting to photograph a pair of these birds at their nest on a heathery island of a Hebridean loch. We rowed out to the island, and when she had seen me into the hide my wife rowed the boat back to the shore. But the crows knew perfectly well that two persons had crossed to the island and that only one had left it, and although I spent a long and weary vigil in the hide the crows would not return to the nest but from time to time flew overhead, 'craa-ing' angrily and suspiciously. That afternoon we played a trick on them, and incidentally proved that they could count. We rowed out again to the island: this time my wife took a watch in the hide and before I rowed the boat back I rigged up a 'dummy' at the stern, complete with cap and oilskins. The crows, seeing two figures leave, concluded that the hide was empty and quickly returned to the nest.

This digression on the grey crow brings to my mind the story of the tame crow which lived as a pet with Alick Grant and his wife and son in Mar Forest.

Alick Grant was deerstalker and piper in that great deer forest: his wife was a Stewart from Atholl (her brother was head stalker in Atholl Forest for many years) and their only son Iain a keen naturalist. When Sandy MacDonald retired from the Derry, Sandy Grant took up his duties as stalker on that beat of the forest and he and his family moved up to the stalker's cottage of Luibeg, just across the river Lui from Derry Lodge. With them they took a pet crow, which had been reared by them as a fledgling a number of years before. The little party crossed the Derry river then, a few hundred yards farther on, crossed the Luibeg stream, and the crow was given its liberty in its new surroundings. A day or two later the settlers crossed once more to the Derry (for the road up the glen does not go farther than that lodge) to bring over their belongings. The crow saw them leave and thinking that their stay in the new home might be only temporary flew with them across the two streams to the Derry. It returned when they returned, and from that day never crossed the streams. It met an untimely fate, being, as was supposed, killed by a weasel. The family mourned their pet, which had been with them for twenty years.

The grey crow is found throughout Europe and I remember noticing that in Russia it was particularly numerous. In that country it was very bold, for it was not apparently molested and fed upon the refuse from the villages. Writing of Russia brings to my mind long sledge journeys through the snow amid interminable forests, the bells of the sleigh ringing cheerily as it was drawn at speed over the frosty ground. In the evenings we would listen to the tuneful singing of sad Russian folk songs. The Russian peasant and the Hebridean crofter would find much in common in their folk music; another link would be their love of hospitality and the friendly evening gatherings which are a feature of both countries.

As the years pass, some of us think back often to old days, and live again happy experiences with friends who have left us. One of my closest friends of those days, Dick Crewe, had a great love for the hills, and many was the walk and the climb we made. Wandering across those lonely and lovely places, a spiritual link was forged between us. After our climbs and walks we used to sit of an evening beside the peat fire of some hill bothy watching the warm glow on the hearth and hearing the hoarse crying of invisible stags in the darkness without. A sense of spiritual one-ness made conversation superfluous on these occasions.

I recall one winter's day a year or two after the passing of my friend when alone I crossed the hill pass we had so often traversed together, and when, throughout that mist-filled walk, I had the sense of his near presence: many people who have walked and lived much alone have had the same experience. Telepathy between the living is more common than many of us realise, but when one of the friends has crossed to another plane the experience is rarer.

Those who are sensitive to the atmosphere of places must have realized that the early Christian saints and holy women have left behind them a spiritual essence which lingers unchanged through the centuries. The atmosphere is felt chiefly upon islands—partly perhaps because small islands are less frequently visited than places on the mainland and these early impressions are thus not rendered faint by more recent ones being super-imposed upon them, but chiefly because the men, and women, of faith of early Christian times had their homes mainly upon islands, where they might without interruption live their simple, holy lives. These islands are sanctified by the strong faith of those who lived long ago here. The power of right thinking does not pass with the passing of those who who have evoked it.

In like manner there are places, and houses, which repel, perhaps because they have some sinister association unknown to him or her who may visit them long after the event that has left its influence. A dark deed may live for centuries in the place where it was enacted. A certain well-known castle which perhaps in fairness it were better that I did not name impressed me strongly with its sinister atmosphere. Here I had an experience which I have often pondered over since. My bedroom was in a distant wing of the castle, where I was quite alone.

The first night I did not sleep too well, but thought little of it; the second night I was more wakeful and uncomfortable and so on the third day decided to eat little for supper and to open my window wide before getting into bed, at the same time drawing back the curtains. Almost at once I fell asleep, but an hour or so after midnight I suddenly awoke, in acute fear. The fire which warmed my room was still burning brightly and therefore the room was not dark, but I felt pressing upon me a great weight, evil and sinister. I felt that the focus of that disquieting presence was at the foot of the bed, but I had not the courage to look in that direction. I lay there miserably, hour after hour, literally counting the leaden minutes as they passed. The warm glow of the fire gave me no comfort: I wished with all my heart that our faithful collie Dileas had been in the room with me; she, I felt, would have sensed the same presence that I had sensed and would have been a comfort to me. At last came the lagging dawn, very faint. A cock crowed somewhere without, and then came a lifting of the weight which had held me imprisoned during the hours of darkness. At once, released from that spell, I fell asleep, and slept soundly until I was called. At breakfast I asked casually whether the castle was haunted. Curious looks were cast at me, and I was asked whether I had had a ghostly experience. I countered that question by asking in turn whether the room in which I had slept had any unpleasant associations and was told that in olden times prisoners were herded into it and were left there before being thrown into the dungeon. I have sometimes wondered since if at certain stages of the night the terror with which that room has been impregnated may in some occult manner be released and whether it was the sensation of ancient fear which I had then experienced. But that would not account for the strong impression I had received that the presence was concentrated at the foot of my bed. I should add that before I visited the castle I had not been told that it was reputedly haunted; this was admitted to me only during the last morning of my stay.

Many, perhaps most, of our old castles have had grim deeds enacted within their walls, but some have a friendly, not a sinister atmosphere. Those who have stayed at Glamis Castle must have sensed this harmonious air. Glamis has its ghost 'The White Lady of Glamis' yet she is friendly and has aroused no feelings of fear in the youthful people who have seen her. The Green Lady of Fyvie Castle is another friendly visitant.

I do not suppose that any really satisfactory explanation will ever be given of ghostly presences, for indeed they may have a variety of origins. The wandering spirit who desires to give utterance to some fervent wish and once that wish had been communicated to a mortal disappears in peace has been recorded in occult happenings times without number. Those persons who believe in reincarnation may suggest that certain haunting spirits have the desire to be born again in human form. That theory of reincarnation might account for many strange experiences —the experience of visiting, apparently for the first time, a place which seems familiar; the experience of meeting a person for the first time and yet feeling one has an old, and perhaps a deep, friendship with that person. There are instances, chiefly from the east, of those who have carried with them into this life experiences of past lives. The materially minded west may dismiss these experiences as delusions, but no one who is able to think for himself can fail to be impressed by some of them. In my own life I have met people with whom I seemed to have this link with the past. Much sadness and joy were mingled in those friendships, but through sadness much is learnt.

Some people have 'a way with them' as the saying goes with children. I am not one of those fortunate persons and therefore when on one occasion a small child attached herself firmly to me I was surprised and also, be it added, pleased. Her grandmother, who was looking after her at the time, said to me, 'It is easy to see that children take a fancy to you.' Quite truthfully I replied that this was not so, and that I had been touched by the affection now shown me. During subsequent months the feeling grew on me, call it a fantasy if you will, but some who read these lines will understand their meaning, that there was a link from a past life between us, something rare and tender and precious. Many of us have found inspiration in Wordsworth's line:

Our birth is but a sleep and a forgetting :
The Soul that rises with us, our life's Star,
Hath had elsewhere its setting,
And cometh from afar :
Not in entire forgetfulness,
And not in utter nakedness,
But trailing clouds of glory do we come
From God, who is our home :
Heaven lies about us in our infancy!

That small child has now grown to girlhood and perhaps remembers nothing of those early days, yet I like to recall them, if only because they were, in Wordsworth's own words, 'Intimations of Immortality'.

It has sometimes been said, and said truly, that in silence a friendship goes deeper than in words. It is in silence that the true harmony of friendship, of love, is felt. In silence there can be created between two souls a one-ness deeper than that forged by talk, by conversation. It has been said that there is in existence somewhere on this earth a kindred soul for each one of us and that on one's journey through life one may, or one may not, meet that kindred spirit; but that he, or she, may be recognised by a sense of one-ness, from which springs the most perfect love—the love that forgets self and for which the highest joy, the greatest privilege, is self-sacrifice. Distance is no barrier to these souls. Through the power of thought they are in communication over land and across oceans, by day or by night; they know faithfully whether the loved one is happy or unhappy. Truly these are the intimations of immortality.

Often in the past when amid the snow-clad peaks and glacier-filled valleys of Spitsbergen I was in communication with my wife, fifteen hundred miles and more distant from me. This interchange of thoughts—telepathy, call it what you will—gives a feeling of power, a feeling of humbleness, a feeling of faith, and one recalls that saying of St. Paul, 'The things which are seen are temporal; the things which are unseen are eternal.'

That spiritual link, tender yet indestructible, which joins two souls is one of the great miracles of life. Through this, the highest expression of human love, the soul is able to reach up to and be sensible of the divine all-embracing love through which the universe has its being.

eptember, in the Western Highlands, sees the culminating glory of the heather—and by the word 'heather' I mean the ling (calluna vulgaris) and not the *ericas*, which flower earlier. On the opening day of the month of September I have walked over the moors of northern Skye, from Kilmuir, where the minister long ago was accustomed to ride to church with his lad, armed with bow and arrow in close attendance, to the shore of Loch Sneosdal, where the *Each Uisge* has his lair. These moors are often dreary because they are almost birdless, but at this time of year they are transformed because of the beauty of the heather. Over the brown moor it seems as though a rich carpet of red has been laid: each fold in the moor, the course of each burn, has been transformed. As I walked over that living carpet the pollen rose as dust from my feet and drifted away upon the wind that blew softly from the Minch. Forgotten are the storms and rains of summer on a day such as this.

It is not only on the moors of Skye that the heather perfume delights the senses. The wind may carry the scent from these moors far across the fields, until the air of the whole island is fragrant. The sun, these fleeting and magic days, is bright and warm and lights up the solan's snowy wing as he makes his unhurried and untiring way above the Minch, fishing as he goes. A friend of mine tells me that he likes best to see the gannet or solan in sunshine against a storm cloud for, he says, one moment the bird seems black as the cloud itself and then, wheeling, gleams white as ivory as its wings catch the sun.

A lover of the ling and its perfume might prolong his pleasure by journeying from place to place throughout the Highlands, for its flowering is later the farther one journeys westward. He might indeed enjoy two heather seasons without travelling far—a journey on foot of fourteen miles, through Lairig Ghru, which separates Glen Derry in Mar Forest from Rothiemurchus Forest in Strathspey. Glen Derry is 1,400 feet above sea level; Rothiemurchus less than 1,000, yet the heather blooms in the former place ten days to a fortnight earlier than in the latter.

On Deeside the ling may be in bloom before August 12th, but at sea level in the Isle of Skye it is the beginning of September before the blossom is at its best and old plants growing in sour, boggy land may not flower until the end of that month. The colour of the flowering ling is said to be purple, but many tones may be found on a moor, from pale pink to a deep and very beautiful rose colour. Some moors have more

white heather than others, but since white heather is greatly prized
and is torn up by the roots by any passer-by, the stock on the more
accessible moorlands has almost vanished.

The common ling is the badge of the Clan Donald.

September flowers are the more precious because of the shortening
days and hints of winter to come. The blue scabious and the pink
bog pimpernel are September blooms. The St. John's wort, Saint
Columba's special plant (to find it unexpectedly was considered by the
Gael to be most fortunate) may be still in flower in early September,
and there are seasons when the globe flower, which is in bloom normally as early as June, may continue to produce flower-heads and
flowers until mid-September, so that the rare sight may be seen beside
some Hebridean stream of ling and globe flower blossoming together.

The twite is a miniature linnet. It is sometimes called the mountain
finch, but this is a misnomer, for it is a bird of the lower moors of
the west. In the Outer Hebrides it is common and in the garden of
Grogary Lodge in the Isle of South Uist several pairs of twites nest each
season, in bushes, or in creepers, or in holes in the dry-stone wall with
which the garden is bounded. The twite makes a dainty nest and as it
rears at least two broods each year the young are sometimes in the nest
at the approach of autumn. One day of late summer a pure white twite
crossed the road ahead of me in northern Skye. It was whiter than the
white chaffinch which was well known and greatly admired in a district
of the Central Highlands. White, or partly white, varieties of the
blackbird are not uncommon, but I have yet to hear of a white thrush.

When I wrote of the well-tended garden at Grogary, of which my
wife and I have pleasant memories, it recalled to me a fine type
of Highlander who laboured for years in our garden. His name was
Norman MacKenzie and what distinguished him from most of his
fellows was his pride in his work. Whatever job he had in hand he put
his whole mind and heart to it, and was not content until it was completed to his satisfaction. He had the soul of an artist, and used to tell
me that he visualised at night when in bed his completed work some
months hence, when flowers would be growing on the bare earth he had
tended so carefully. Anything Norman turned his hand to he did well. In
his younger days he had been a fisherman and had sailed in the herring
fleet before the days of motors. He had more skill in fashioning sea-
fishing lines than any man I have known, but there seemed to be
nothing he could not make. If you asked him to build you a wheel-

barrow it was done perfectly, well-finished and durable. No less skilled was he in making a fence, or the model of a sailing vessel. Whatever he created he looked upon with pride, even with love—that was one of the secrets of the beauty of his work.

He came with me to St. Kilda, when the people still inhabited that island, and he lodged with one of the natives, while MacLeod's factor and I put up at another house. One morning he told me that his host the evening before had asked him if he would fancy a puffin for his supper. The puffin was boiled for no longer than a quarter of an hour and was then served. Although Norman had the strongest teeth of any man I have known—he used them habitually to untie a knot in a rope so tight that his fingers were unable to loosen it—he said that the puffin beat him, and that he was unable to 'make anything of it' with his teeth. He told me that his 'landlord', as he called the St. Kildan, kept saying to him, in Gaelic of course, 'Is not this the fine bird?' and that he was agreeing with him for the sake of good manners, although there was little headway he could make with it.

Norman had many stories of earlier days. One which he liked to tell was of a supper party given by a West Highland landowner to some old men who had been helping him to make improvements to the estate. All went well until the end of supper, when cigars were brought in. The host did not smoke, and none of the worthies had ever seen a cigar before. Each looked at the other in doubt, then one of the *bodachan* had a brain wave—he picked up his cigar and began to eat it—and the others promptly followed suit!

I remember Norman's love of pipe music and how I often played to him on the pipes. As September is, or was in peacetime, the month of Highland Gatherings, I may here say something of the great pipers of the present day. The war abruptly put an end to the Highland Gatherings, and pipers, as I write at the beginning of 1944, are scattered throughout the world. For a good many years now I have helped to adjudicate at the piping competitions at the various Highland meetings —not only in the Highlands, for the Highland Pipers' Society of London held annually their competition in that city—and it has been my good fortune to know all the leading pipers during the last quarter of a century. The average Englishman, I suppose, regards the Highland bagpipe as an instrument which emits an unpleasant sound and which it takes no great musical ability to play. But the truth is far otherwise. The greatest composers of bagpipe music of all times were the MacCrimmons of Skye, they who were hereditary pipers to the MacLeods of Dunvegan, and who had their piping college at Boreraig, on the shore of Loch Dunvegan. It was a saying of the MacCrimmons that in the making of a piper it took seven years of piping and seven generations of piping ancestors. There may be poetic licence in that saying but it is certain that the MacCrimmons insisted on their pupils practising harder, and over a longer period, than is customary at the present time. I have heard the story that MacCrimmon would write down a tune on the wet sand as the tide began to ebb, and would expect his pupils to be able to play it before the flood tide once more flowed over the sand and washed away the marks.

So far as is known the MacCrimmons taught only the Ceòl Mór, or Big Music—that is the classical pipe music in which their compositions, made centuries ago, are still pre-eminent. Ceòl Mór is usually known as Piobaireachd at the present day, and there is a competition in Piobaireachd at all the great Highland Gatherings. In the language of music a Piobaireachd may be termed a recitative sonata: from the theme, which is usually slow and solemn, different variations are built up, culminating in the fast, intricate movement, the Crunluadh, with its doubling and trebling.

The general impression that a Piobaireachd is always a Lament is erroneous. The composition may, it is true, be a Lament, but it may also be a Salute, a Gathering, a Taunt or Satire, or a measure (such as MacLeod of MacLeod's Rowing Piobaireachd) composed to keep the rowers of the chief's *birlinn* or galley together—the sense of time in a measure of this kind is very pronounced.

A short Piobaireachd takes ten minutes to play: one of the longest, as it is one of the most lovely, the Lament for Donald Bàn MacCrimmon (he who was slain at the Rout of Moy) takes from eighteen to twenty minutes. One of the best renderings of this tune that I have heard was at the Argyllshire Gathering, in the Gold Medal competition, by Malcolm (Calum) MacPherson, son of Angus MacPherson of Invershin and grandson of the finest piper of his day, Calum MacPherson, piper to Cluny MacPherson. Malcolm of the present generation is, at his best, a very fine player indeed.[1]

I received most of my tuition in Piobaireachd from John MacDonald, Inverness, he who has held the appointment of Honorary Piper to the King during the last two reigns. It is, I think, universally conceded that John MacDonald is pre-eminent among living pipers. A leading

[1] Another outstanding performance I recall was the playing of 'The Lament for the Children' by Pipe Major G. S. MacLennan at the Skye Highland Gathering in 1926.

amateur piper of the day once said to me, 'If I had practised hard all my life I believe that my playing might have equalled the playing of the leading professionals of the day, all except John MacDonald: his playing I could never hope to equal.' What is the secret of John MacDonald's piping—that magic touch which is denied to all others? Pennant, almost 200 years ago, wrote of MacArthur, hereditary piper to MacDonald of the Isles, that 'he was quite master of his instrument', and I think that the same remark might be made of John MacDonald at the present day. I can imagine the MacCrimmons being as good as John MacDonald in their playing, but I can imagine no piper excelling him. In him are combined perfect fingering, perfect timing and beautiful expression, the whole producing a rare and very lovely harmony that thrills the senses. It is the hall-mark of genius that it should all sound so simple—the listener feels there is no reason why he should not go home and do the same thing himself. When John MacDonald ends his playing days (and he is getting 'up in years' as the Highland saying goes) something rare and precious will be lost in piping.

It is a strange commentary on the recognition of genius that John MacDonald should have been asked to broadcast on two occasions only, although other pipers are approached regularly by the B.B.C. One of these broadcasts was an Empire Broadcast, and made therefore in the very early hours of the morning. I had been asked to give a brief description of the tunes he would play so John and I arrived at the studio an hour after midnight and were joined by a friend who was a great lover of pipe music. When the red light went up for the broadcast to begin, the announcer, perhaps wearied by the labours of the day and knowing little or nothing of the man he was to announce, made a bad start by telling listeners throughout the Empire that they would 'now hear Piper MacLeod'. This mistake in the name would have had an adverse effect on some musicians, yet with John it was otherwise, and in that hot and stuffy studio, within a chalked circle marked 'Piper', he there and then played that great MacCrimmon composition 'I got a kiss of the King's Hand'. He played the *Urlar* or groundwork, and as variation followed variation the spell of his playing seized the heart and mind. Came the Crunluadh, its doubling and trebling, the intricate grace notes played to perfection, so that the studio was filled with a flood of harmony, with a rippling as of waves upon the seashore. I have heard John's playing so many times that I have become attuned to its exellence, yet I think that on that occasion he excelled himself. A tribute to his playing that night I recall. My friend after a time rose from his seat in the studio and, with his hand shading his eyes, paced slowly after the piper, as though joined

Herring Gull attacking the author.

Herring Gull just after its attack

Outpost of the old Caledonian Forest.

to him by an invisible thread, for he was held fast in the spell of that master playing.

As we all walked home in the early hours of the morning I ventured to say to the announcer, 'It was a pity you did not get his name right.' It was a mild remark, yet when he had left us John turned to me and said, 'It was a pity you said that; you might have hurt his feelings'!

If John MacDonald competed at a Highland Gathering it was a foregone conclusion that he would win the competition, and I recall that on one occasion at the Northern Meeting, when he played 'Lament for King James', his fellow competitors joined in the applause which came at the end of his playing: yet to hear him at his best one had to be in his own home, and after my lesson I would sometimes induce him to play. I have memories of his piping of 'The Earl of Antrim', 'Lament for Donald Bàn', and the 'Children's Lament'. These were among the great musical experiences of my life. Of him it might be said: 'He feels that only the best is worth an effort, but that this is worth all effort,' as Grey wrote in appraising the great qualities of Morley.

It has sometimes been said of John MacDonald that he is King of Pipers. His kingly qualities are shown not only in the unrivalled excellence of his playing of the old classical pipe music, for in his daily life he has been an inspiration to me and to many others—in his scrupulous honour and integrity, his courtesy, dignity and kindliness, and in the calm, serene, manner in which he has taken the blows of fate, the vicissitudes of fortune.

If John MacDonald is the uncrowned king of piping in its classical form, William Ross is its greatest champion in its lighter side—in the playing of March, Strathspey and Reel—sometimes known as Ceòl Beag, Little Music, as compared with the Piobaireachd or Ceòl Mór. William Ross was formerly Pipe Major in the Scots Guards and saw much active service. Since the year 1919 he has been the Piobaireachd Society's Instructor and has presided at the College of Piping at Edinburgh Castle. To this college or school the War Office sends the most promising army pipers, and a constant stream of players, not only from Britain but from all parts of the Empire, are passing through his hands. The strain of carrying on, single-handed, this important class, day after day, year after year, must be great. Yet the instructor's enthusiasm remains, and many is the piper who is proud to have been present at a course under this great pipe major. Pipe Major Ross comes of a talented musical family and owes much of his success to the encouragement given him throughout his life by his mother who (1944) although beyond the fourscore years is still active and vigorous.

The older school of pipers are passing from us, and few remain. Unique in his enthusiasm for the Ceòl Mór is that accomplished player and true Highlander, Angus MacPherson of Invershin, Sutherland. Each time that I pass his door I receive the old-fashioned Highland welcome and many is the beautiful composition I have heard Angus play beside the waters of the Shin, where silvery salmon leaped from the brown, peat-stained water as though aroused by his playing.

There are many other fine pipers, all of whom cannot be mentioned here. Few of the great competitions have been decided without the name of Robert Reid appearing in the prize list. Two of the King's pipers at Balmoral—now both on active service and pipe majors—are Robert Brown and Robert Nicol. Pupils of John MacDonald, they have learnt deeply of the lore of piping and may be able to carry on the tradition of their great master. Before Robert Brown became the celebrated piper he now is he was on one occasion competing at the Braemar Gathering. I was on that occasion one of the judges of the piping events, and His Majesty King George V asked me what I thought of the playing of a new piper of his, named Brown. I happened to know how greatly Brown wished to have a course of tuition under John MacDonald, and replied that Brown was good but would be even better if it could be arranged that he went to John MacDonald. 'But', said the King, 'I can't spare him: he trapped three thousand rabbits for me last winter.' 'Well sir,' I replied, greatly daring, 'I would rather have a piper who had been under John MacDonald than a man who trapped 3,000 rabbits.' The King smiled in his kindly, homely way. 'Perhaps you are right,' he said; 'I will see that Brown goes to John MacDonald.' That was the beginning of the tuition Brown and Nicol received under John MacDonald, and I am sure no pipers more deeply appreciated the privilege of that tuition.

Pipe Major MacDonald has had many pupils, yet I doubt whether any of them has succeeded in emulating his magic touch. One of his latest pupils, Pipe Major Donald MacLeod of the Seaforth Highlanders, I heard in the late summer of 1942, and in his playing I seemed to hear an echo of John MacDonald's.

At the present day there are more pipers than ever before, yet the master touch seems to be disappearing. As John MacDonald once said to me 'Piobaireachd is dying'. I think that the reason for this is the speed at which modern life is lived, and now that scarcely a Highland chief retains his piper (I except Lochiel, whose piper Norman MacRae has been with him for forty years and still retains the excellence of his playing) the tradition of Highland piping, apart from army piping, has been almost lost. The MacCrimmons were the greatest pipers of all times, but they were encouraged by their chief and patron, MacLeod, from whom they held their lands rent-free. MacCrimmon was a person of importance; he had always a lad whose duty it was to carry his pipe, or to bring him the instrument before he played upon it. He lived in a day before the Highlands and Islands were depopulated by emigration, and by migration to the towns and cities, and when there were few distractions to prevent him perfecting his art.

In an earlier chapter I recorded that birds and animals were fast becoming air-minded and now ignore the great mechanical birds which easily outstrip their best speed. There are still exceptions to this general rule. The barnacle goose which nests in Greenland and Spitsbergen and winters on grassy uninhabited islands of the Hebrides, mistrusts aircraft as much as ever. Lobster fishermen who lift their creels round these islands tell me that if an aircraft should pass near, the geese rise in alarm; when a succession of planes appear the alarm becomes a panic. But these birds are the exception.

I recall the now almost classical story of the aircraft (this was in the earlier days of flying) travelling at approximately ninety miles an hour, which was overtaken by a golden eagle flying on the same course. The pilot saw the eagle eye the aircraft with calm indifference before it slowly drew ahead of him. There are instances, too, of birds nesting on the grass of aerodromes, unperturbed by the planes which are almost constantly around and above them. I heard of a lapwing or green plover which made its nest and laid its four eggs right in the track of taking-off bombers. In the end that bird became so tame that she would allow a bomber to roar taxi-ing over her without rising from the nest. Aerodromes indeed attract birds because the grass is kept short and green here, and this permits ground-feeding birds to find food without difficulty.[1]

In September, after their nesting cares have ended, birds of prey turn against their young ones and drive them ruthlessly from the parental nesting territory. These refugees sometimes wander far from the land of their birth. A buzzard was once sent me by a kind-hearted person who

[1] On one aerodrome in Scotland a number of pairs of lesser terns nest.

had taken it from a trap—if I remember rightly—and nursed it back to health. My correspondent thought that if it were liberated in his district of the south the bird would probably be shot or again trapped, and since he knew that Skye was a favourite haunt of the buzzard he asked me if I would see that it was released there. The bird duly arrived, and was liberated on the coast a couple of miles from our house. It had perhaps been kept too long in captivity in its previous quarters and had forgotten how to earn its own living. It soon made itself unpopular by preying upon the crofters' chickens, and since it was known that the bird had been sent to us to be released we began to feel an unwelcome responsibility for it. The buzzard then turned its attentions to our own chickens and was so bold that it squeezed itself through the opening in the wire-netting run in which the chickens were kept. This happened several times, and the bird on each occasion succeeded in making its escape before it was caught. A little later, when my wife and I were from home, the buzzard again inserted itself into the chicken run. The cook heard the shriek of a chicken which it was murdering, seized a poker (the first thing that came to her hand) rushed out, and succeeded in getting between the bird and the exit to the run. She then entered the enclosure, stalked the buzzard with the poker and after, we were assured, a desperate struggle, killed it. That buzzard had lost its fear of man, and even if it had escaped and had succeeeded in finding a mate, would never have left the chickens of the district alone, for it had learnt how to obtain food without difficulty.

Another wanderer was the shearwater which one September day presumably came down the chimney of a house which stands near a West Highland sea loch. The human occupants were from home at the time and when they returned my friend's wife heard a scratching noise under the piano late in the evening. Investigations were made and a Manx shearwater in an exhausted state was found. The right wing and right leg of the bird appeared to be injured and it was unable to fly. The visitor was placed in a box of hay near an electric radiator that night and next morning seemed better. After resting for two days the captive was livelier on the third morning and bit my friend's hand. By inducing it to repeat the biting, means were found of feeding the bird, for when it gripped the human hand its bill was half open and food could be inserted into it. This was a slow process, and a painful one for the owner of the hand! Diet consisted of small pieces of herring, brown trout and mussels. Latterly it was found that small pieces of raw beef did the bird most good. After its meal the shearwater was dropped into a butt of water, where it swam and cleaned itself. It loved the warmth of a coat or jersey and found pleasure in burrowing down the sleeve, chirping and chortling with satisfaction.

When the invalid had recovered it was carried to the shore and placed in a small sandy pool as the tide was coming in. The shearwater swam round, then tried a flight, which was successful, and after an elaborate toilet and apparently a feed amongst the seaweed, was last seen farther out on the loch.

I have elsewhere mentioned the shearwater—a true oceanic bird—which was found dead in the very heart of the Central Highlands. The storms of autumn are often severe, birds are blown off their course, and over land a sea bird is in as bad a plight as a land bird is at sea.

There are those who insist that the weather of the Western Highlands and Islands is more stormy than it was. All the older generation agree on this, and some of them believe that the time of the 'Black Rains' foretold by the Brahan Seer has come. The 'Black Rains', it was prophesied, would inundate the land, and would cause the people to emigrate. Those who believe in this prophesy point to the evacuation of St. Kilda and the Monach Islands as the beginning of that emigration. It is true that recent years have seen unusually prolonged periods of bad weather, that in the years 1941, 1942, and 1943, there was no real summer in the west, the oat crop was harvested in October and November, and the potatoes after that.[1] But the weather experts tell us that while we may indeed be living in a wet and stormy cycle there has been no real change in the climate. They say that old people remember the unusual years of their youth, not the usual years. They remember, simply because it *was* unusual, a winter of frost and snow, and a summer of sunshine and heat, but they do *not* remember the winters of wind and rain, nor the summers of rain and mist. As a proof of this they point to old records and old writings; to the statement made in the Statistical Account of Skye, published more than a century ago. Here the writer (the Parish Minister) puts it on record that old people then affirmed that when they were young the winters were colder, and the summers drier and warmer, than when the account was written—and this is exactly what a Parish Minister would write at the present day!

In the West the weather changes so suddenly and unexpectedly that weather prophets have a bad time and I have met few indeed who have vindicated themselves. One of these was a farmer who had an almost uncanny prescience in weather matters. I remember one evening at sunset after a cloudless, calm day asking him what the conditions the

[1] There has so far (mid June) been no summer in 1944.

next morning would be. 'Wind and rain' he made answer. The barometer was high and steady, the weather apparently set-fair, yet he was
right—the next day was a very bad one. There is one thing that the
meteorologist soon discovers in the west—the height of the barometer
has very little to do with the weather. I recall a fisherman saying once
to me on a fine winter day with an unusually high glass, 'The weather
looks well, but I don't like the glass; IT'S TOO HIGH.' I remember thinking that if someone, say in the Midlands of England, had heard that
remark they would have been surprised, to say the least of it. But it was
an apt one, for the next day, although the barometer remained at set-
fair, a full gale with rain swept the coast. The explanation of this bad
weather with a high glass is that the Hebrides and the western mainland
lie sometimes at the edge of a great anticyclone or fine weather system
which embraces the British Isles. There are then usually a series of de-
pressions passing on a north-easterly track between Scotland and Iceland, and it is they which, although distant, influence the weather in the
west rather than the anticyclone. But it is safe to say that, so long as the
wind is in the south west, the weather will remain unsettled in the
west. With this wind the great rains of the wet western districts fall—
for instance that exceptional monthly fall of 29·5 inches at Loan in
Lochaber in October, 1943. There are certain signs that tell the
weather student what he may expect during the following twelve, or
perhaps twenty-four hours.

A sunrise when the clouds are suffused with red almost to the zenith
is a sure sign of bad weather to follow The old proverb that a
sunrise of this kind is the shepherd's warning is well known. What is
less well known is that a green sky (I speak of the west, for I have
found that weather portents in the east do not always agree with those
in the west) is an almost sure sign of rain. The day, let us say, has been
fine, but toward sunset the blue sky takes on a greenish tinge and in it a
few grey smoke-like clouds are born and float with little motion. This
green sky may be visible in only one direction—toward the horizon in
the north west, let us say, or perhaps to the south east. This sign, nine
times out of ten, means that rain will follow within the next twelve
hours.

A halo round the sun is generally a sign of an approaching storm: it is a
signal that a new depression is advancing upon the Hebrides from the
Atlantic. In summer, however, this 'ring round the sun' as it is popu-
larly described, may be the forerunner of heat. A good many years ago
now my wife and I were camping beside an Outer Hebridean loch. We

arrived at the tail end of a long spell of wet weather, which gave place to a fine sunny day with a very obvious ring round the sun. I had little doubt that this signified more bad weather to follow; instead it ushered in one of the finest and hottest spells known in the Outer Isles, with continuous sun and a shade temperature in the 80s. I heard since from old weather prophets that a ring round the sun did sometimes come before a fine weather spell. A remarkable solar halo was witnessed by me, and by a good many other people, on July 1, 1943. In addition to a ring round the sun of normal circumference, a vast circle, white and ghostly, intersected it and stretched away to the north-west heavens although the morning sun was in the south east at the time.

A parhelion or mock sun is almost always a sign of unsettled weather. Solar halos and mock suns are caused by the sun's rays being deflected by ice particles floating at an immense height in the atmosphere.

When the hills look near, lofty, and a deep blue, it is a sign of a weather change: when they are clear and apparently of no great height it is a sign of fine weather. When the air is clear and a curtain of haze spreads over the sky from the south it is a sign that the south wind will arise. When the isles are lifted up a little way above the ocean's surface by refraction it is a sign of north wind.

Sometimes, but rarely, in hot fine weather the hills of the Outer Isles as seen from the north-west wing of Skye change shape. They grow miraculously in size, become flat-topped where before they were conical, and the observer could be forgiven if he felt that here he was indeed in an enchanted land. On certain rare days I have seen the hills of the Outer Isles so transformed that even one most familiar with them would have failed to recognise them. This phenomenon is not a mirage, but it is perhaps akin to it.

Some living creatures know the signs of the weather. On a fine evening, after a dry hot spell, if the large black slug is abroad the observer can be confident that rain will follow.

If the river be full of fresh-run salmon, which leap from the water yet refuse to take the most skilfully thrown fly, it is a sign that a change in the weather is near.

Red deer are good weather prophets. If deer in the early morning begin to feed out on to the high ground it is a sign of a fine day. If they have been for some time on the higher hills and begin to come down to the glen it is a sign that the fine weather is near its close.

September of late years has brought wind and rain and a numbing cold. I have seen the hills of Harris rise white to the heavens on a recent September morning and biting hail and snow squalls shake the ripening oats, which were flattened by the wind before they were ready to be harvested.

But let us hope that the spell of bad summers is nearing its end.

In a letter to a friend of mine that great naturalist, W. H. Hudson, wrote that he was never really happy over one of his books, not even *Far Away and Long Ago*, which critics called his best. He said that *Green Mansions* was not a great work, though there was a good idea at the bottom of it—which he thought came out only in the last part of the work, after Rima had gone.

It is perhaps not a good sign that an author should be satisfied with what he creates for, if his aim is high, he is striving toward the unattainable. His greatest hope may be (as mine has been) to paint his word pictures, so that his readers may see something of the beauty he has seen, and that their minds may be refreshed by the beauty and the divine essence which may be discerned in Nature by him who has the eyes to see beyond the material to the inner being of pure spirit.

With these thoughts I leave my *Highland Year* and send it forth into the world from the lonely Isle of Skye.